# GOD NEVER GIVES UP ON YOU

# ALSO BY MAX LUCADO

## INSPIRATIONAL

3:16
A Gentle Thunder
A Love Worth Giving
And the Angels Were Silent
Anxious for Nothing
Because of Bethlehem
Before Amen
Come Thirsty
Cure for the Common Life
Facing Your Giants
Fearless
Glory Days
God Came Near
Grace
Great Day Every Day
He Chose the Nails
He Still Moves Stones
Help Is Here
How Happiness Happens
In the Eye of the Storm
In the Grip of Grace
It's Not About Me
Just Like Jesus
Max on Life
More to Your Story
Next Door Savior
No Wonder They Call
   Him the Savior
On the Anvil
Outlive Your Life
Six Hours One Friday
The Applause of Heaven
The Great House of God
Traveling Light
Unshakable Hope
When Christ Comes
When God Whispers
   Your Name
You Are Never Alone
You'll Get Through This
You Were Made for
   This Moment

## COMPILATIONS

Begin Again
In the Footsteps of
   the Savior
Jesus
Start with Prayer
They Walked with God

## FICTION

Christmas Stories
Miracle at the Higher
   Grounds Café
The Christmas Candle

## BIBLES (GENERAL EDITOR)

Children's Daily
   Devotional Bible
Grace for the Moment
   Daily Bible
The Lucado Encouraging
   Word Bible
The Lucado Life Lessons
   Study Bible

## CHILDREN'S BOOKS

A Max Lucado
   Children's Treasury
Anxious for Nothing
   (Young Readers
   Edition)
Bedtime Prayers for
   Little Ones
God Always Keeps
   His Promises
God Forgives Me, and
   I Forgive You
Grace for the Moment:
   365 Devotions
   for Kids
Hermie, a Common
   Caterpillar
I'm Not a Scaredy Cat
Itsy Bitsy Christmas

Just in Case You
   Ever Wonder
Lucado Treasury of
   Bedtime Prayers
One Hand, Two Hands
Thank You, God, for
   Blessing Me
Thank You, God,
   for Loving Me
The Crippled Lamb
The Oak Inside the Acorn
You Can Count on God:
   100 Devotions for Kids
Where'd My Giggle Go?

## YOUNG ADULT BOOKS

3:16
It's Not About Me
Make Every Day Count
Unshakable Hope
   Promise Book
Wild Grace
You Were Made to
   Make a Difference

## GIFT BOOKS

Fear Not Promise Book
For the Tough Times
God Thinks You're
   Wonderful
Grace for the Moment
Grace Happens Here
Happy Today
His Name Is Jesus
Let the Journey Begin
Live Loved
Mocha with Max
Safe in the Shepherd's
   Arms
This Is Love
You Changed My Life

# GOD NEVER GIVES UP ON YOU

WHAT JACOB'S STORY TEACHES
US ABOUT GRACE, MERCY, AND
GOD'S RELENTLESS LOVE

## MAX LUCADO

THOMAS NELSON
Since 1798

*God Never Gives Up on You*

Published in Nashville, Tennessee, by Thomas Nelson. Thomas Nelson is a registered trademark of HarperCollins Christian Publishing, Inc.

Thomas Nelson titles may be purchased in bulk for educational, business, fundraising, or sales promotional use. For information please e-mail SpecialMarkets@ThomasNelson.com.

Unless otherwise noted, Scripture quotations are taken from the New King James Version®. Copyright © 1982 by Thomas Nelson. Used by permission. All rights reserved.

Scripture quotations marked AMPC are from the Amplified® Bible (AMPC). Copyright © 1954, 1958, 1962, 1964, 1965, 1987 by The Lockman Foundation. Used by permission. www.Lockman.org. Scripture quotations marked ESV are from the ESV® Bible (The Holy Bible, English Standard Version®). Copyright © 2001 by Crossway, a publishing ministry of Good News Publishers. Used by permission. All rights reserved. Scripture quotations marked THE MESSAGE are from The Message. Copyright © 1993, 2002, 2018 by Eugene H. Peterson. Used by permission of NavPress. All rights reserved. Represented by Tyndale House Publishers, a Division of Tyndale House Ministries. Scripture quotations marked NASB are from the New American Standard Bible® (NASB). Copyright © 1960, 1962, 1963, 1968, 1971, 1972, 1973, 1975, 1977, 1995, 2020 by the Lockman Foundation. Used by permission. www.Lockman.org. Scripture quotations marked NCV are from the New Century Version®. Copyright © 2005 by Thomas Nelson. Used by permission. All rights reserved. Scripture quotations marked NIV are from the Holy Bible, New International Version®, NIV®. Copyright © 1973, 1978, 1984, 2011 by Biblica, Inc.® Used by permission of Zondervan. All rights reserved worldwide. www.zondervan.com. The "NIV" and "New International Version" are trademarks registered in the United States Patent and Trademark Office by Biblica, Inc.® Scripture quotations marked NLT are from the Holy Bible, New Living Translation. Copyright © 1996, 2004, 2015 by Tyndale House Foundation. Used by permission of Tyndale House Ministries, Carol Stream, Illinois 60188. All rights reserved. Scripture quotations marked PHILLIPS are from The New Testament in Modern English by J. B. Phillips. Copyright © 1960, 1972 J. B. Phillips. Administered by The Archbishops' Council of the Church of England. Used by permission. Scripture quotations marked RSV are from the Revised Standard Version of the Bible. Copyright 1946, 1952, and 1971 National Council of the Churches of Christ in the United States of America. Used by permission. All rights reserved. Scripture quotations marked TLB are from The Living Bible. Copyright © 1971. Used by permission of Tyndale House Publishers, a Division of Tyndale House Ministries, Carol Stream, Illinois 60188. All rights reserved. Scripture quotations marked WNT are from the Weymouth New Testament. Public domain.

Any internet addresses, phone numbers, or company or product information printed in this book are offered as a resource and are not intended in any way to be or to imply an endorsement by Thomas Nelson, nor does Thomas Nelson vouch for the existence, content, or services of these sites, phone numbers, companies, or products beyond the life of this book.

ISBN 978-1-4002-3956-6 (audiobook)
ISBN 978-1-4002-3954-2 (eBook)
ISBN 978-1-4002-3957-3 (IE)
ISBN 978-1-4002-3953-5 (HC)

**Library of Congress Cataloging-in-Publication Data**

Names: Lucado, Max, author.
Title: God never gives up on you : what Jacob's story teaches us about grace, mercy, and God's relentless love / Max Lucado.
Description: Nashville, Tennessee : Thomas Nelson, [2023] | Summary: "Ever wonder if you've had one too many stumbles for God to use someone like you? If you could benefit from a tale of God's unending, unbending, unswerving love and devotion, let bestselling author and pastor Max Lucado show you how God's grace will transform your life"-- Provided by publisher.
Identifiers: LCCN 2022049125 (print) | LCCN 2022049126 (ebook) | ISBN 9781400239566 (audiobook) | ISBN 9781400239535 (hc) | ISBN 9781400239542 (ebook) | ISBN 9781400239573 (IE)
Subjects: LCSH: Jacob (Biblical patriarch)--Biblical teaching. | Grace (Theology)
Classification: LCC BS580.J3 L78 2023 (print) | LCC BS580.J3 (ebook) | DDC 222/.1106--dc23/eng/20230503
LC record available at https://lccn.loc.gov/2022049125
LC ebook record available at https://lccn.loc.gov/2022049126

*Printed in the United States of America*

23 24 25 26 27 LBC 5 4 3 2 1

*With joy Denalyn and I dedicate this book to Travis and Alisha Eades and their children: Jackson, Landon, Weston, and Annie. They walk with God, lead with faith, and worship with glad hearts. We are honored to serve alongside them.*

# CONTENTS

# ACKNOWLEDGMENTS

A VOLUME OF THANKS WOULD NOT BE ENOUGH to express my gratitude for the team behind this book. They dedicate themselves to the creation of quality messages and books. To them, I happily offer a standing ovation.

Liz Heaney and Karen Hill—editors who coax this stubborn mule of an author to clean up phrases and tighten up paragraphs.

Carol Bartley—the best copy editor on the planet.

David Drury—a theological safeguard against wayward thoughts.

Steve, Cheryl, and Caroline Green—dearest of friends and most faithful of workers.

The HCCP Publishing team—Mark Schoenwald, Don Jacobson, Andrew Stoddard, Mark Glesne, Erica Smith, Bria Woods, Janene MacIvor, and Laura Minchew.

Greg, Susan, and Andrew Ligon—captains who keep this boat afloat and on target.

The Dunham Group—so thankful for your timely and creative ideas.

Dave Treat—prayer leader and Christ-lover.

Jana Muntsinger and Pamela McClure—publicists who can leap buildings with a single bound.

Janie Padilla and Margaret Mechinus—steady and dependable. Thank you!

Andrea Lucado Ramsay—more than a daughter, a coworker. Great work, Dre!

Brett, Jenna, Rosie, Max, Rob, Andrea, Jeff, and Sara—you occupy a place in this Papa's heart that is all yours. Love you forever.

Denalyn, my bride—though it's been well over four decades since our wedding, never will I forget the sight of you walking down the aisle. I saw your smile, and that's the last I've seen of my heart.

You, the reader—if you choose to entrust me with your time, I will do my best to honor your trust. God bless you.

And to you, my Holy Father, I offer the greatest thanks. I, like Jacob, am inconsistent and forgetful. Yet I, like Jacob, am secured by the strong hand of heaven's grace. And I am forever grateful.

# CHAPTER 1

# THE TILTED HALO SOCIETY

**IF YOU ARE A SUPERSAINT, THIS BOOK IS NOT** for you. If your halo never tilts, your faith never wavers, your Bible never closes, and your feet never stray from the straight and narrow, let me save you some time. You won't relate to this story.

Are you squeaky clean? Is this your only question about faith? Why would people question their faith? Is your heart so fully set on heaven that you use Pearlygate.com as your email address? Do you begin your day with an "Our Father" and end your day with an "Amen" and never interrupt the prayer?

If so, congratulations! My hat is off to you. Here is a standing ovation. And here is an honest disclaimer: these chapters were not written with the likes of you in mind.

This book is for members of the Tilted Halo Society. For

3

strugglers among us and the fumbler within us. For those of us who are part saint, part scoundrel. We mean well, but do well? Well, we don't always. We have breakthroughs, for sure, but breakdowns as well, often in the same hour. We need no reminder of our failures. We have not forgotten them. But we could use a refresher course on God's stubborn refusal to give up on us.

And no one is more suited to the task than Jacob, the flawed patriarch.

He is, by definition, a patriarch. Yet in the team photo of Bible heroes, he looks out of place. There stand Abraham and Isaac with their rush of hair, strong shoulders, and chiseled features. Mount Rushmore-ish, they are. Then there's Jacob, the little guy wearing the sunglasses and poker visor. He doesn't seem to fit.

Jacob's nickname contains the same consonants as the Hebrew word for *heel*. Appropriate, as he exited the womb with a hand on his twin brother's heel as if to say, "Oh, no you don't, you fuzzy brother. I want the top spot." A triumph of irony, this was: Jacob beginning life the way he would live it, grasping for a better position. Jacob's nickname was Deceiver, and deceive he did.[1] He took advantage of his famished sibling, pulled the wool over the eyes of his dying father, and met his father-in-law's guile with guile.

Prodigy? No. Prodigal? That fits. Jacob never fed the pigs, but he did wrestle in the mud with, if not God, Someone like God. All night the two grunted, gripped, and groped until, as the day broke, Jacob pinned him down and begged for a blessing. The blessing came but at a cost. Jacob was given a new name: Israel. But Israel's hip was out of joint.

He walked with a limp.

Sound familiar? You've wrestled with God about your past, your future, your pain and problems. You, like Jacob, have walked away with a gimp in your spiritual gait. Some people mount up with wings like eagles, a few run and never grow weary, others walk and never faint.[2]

You? Me? Jacob? We limp.

Jacob's story is for limpers.

I spoke with a limper last evening. We sat together at a dinner party. A dozen folks shared a meal, a bottle of wine, and a gorgeous South Texas sunset. The husbands sat outside on a backyard deck. I was the newcomer. "What kind of work are you in, Max?" I winced at the question. Nothing dampens lively conversation more quickly than the discovery of a clergyman in the circle. (Confession: when I'm on a flight and am asked about my profession, my answer depends on my energy level. If I'm in a mood to chat, I say "writer." If not, I say "preacher.")

"Well, I'm a pastor." Silence. The supersaints at the table (there is usually one or two) shared news about their Bible study in which they have learned so much. The limpers (there are always several) apologized for their language and made a joke about passing the offering plate after dessert.

The chitchat resumed, but the fellow to my right, in a voice intended for my ears only, began to talk about his faith, or lack thereof. If he wasn't eighty years old in age, he certainly was in appearance. His eyelids drooped to half-mast; his shoulders slumped. He puffed on a cigar and sipped on a glass of pinot noir. His uncle, he told me, was a pastor. The uncle had baptized him in an Alabama river. But that was seven decades ago. He's buried a child since then, buried some dreams as well. He's built and lost a business or two since then. He's wrestled with God since then. "I guess I'm God's lost cause," he said.

He would find a kindred spirit in Jacob.

Jacob's story is hard to read because he misbehaved so often. Then again, the Jacob story is a relief to read because we misbehave so often. We wonder, *If God could love and use Jacob, might he be willing to do the same with us?*

Jacob lived 147 years.[3] Yet the heart of his narrative covers only twenty years of his life (ages seventy-seven to ninety-seven)[4] and eleven chapters in the book of Genesis (25–35). We know very little about Jacob's life outside of those twenty years. But what we know of those two decades is worth pondering.

The setting is southern Israel some two thousand years before Jesus was born. The main characters are bedouins: tent dwellers and sheep watchers. The land about them is vast and rugged. Their story is a multilayered mosaic that begins with Jacob's grandfather.

Abraham was wealthy in herds and flocks, silver and gold. He was also affluent in faith, so rich, in fact, that he set out from his homeland in search of a new land that would serve as the heartland of a new nation.[5]

His faith allowed for a new nation but not a new baby. When God told Abraham and his wife, Sarah, it was time to buy a stroller and decorate a nursery, they cracked up. Abraham was pushing a hundred years of age; she was nigh on ninety. The thought of bouncing a baby on bony knees left them in stitches.[6] She made a joke about parents and child being equally toothless. Abraham agreed, "We'll all be wearing diapers!" He fell on his face in a fit of laughter, and she giggled herself into a knot.

But the baby came. They named him Chuckles. Well, not exactly, but they might as well have because Isaac means "laugh,"[7] proof that when it comes to miracles, God has the last laugh.

In his later years Abraham decided to find Chuckles a wife. Abraham sent a servant back to the land of his birth to "get a wife for my son" (Gen. 24:4 NIV). The servant prayed for God to grant him success. He'd hardly said an "amen" when he looked up and saw Rebekah, Isaac's wife-to-be. The servant sought the blessing of Rebekah's father and the permission of her brother. The brother was named Laban. Remember that name. In short order he will trick Jacob, who had just tricked his father, Isaac, and his brother, Esau. Lots of tricking in this story.

Laban gave Rebekah to the servant.

The servant gave Rebekah to Isaac.

Isaac gave his heart to Rebekah.

And Rebekah gave twin sons, Jacob and Esau, to Isaac.

There was tension between the brothers from the get-go. Rebekah's womb felt like a cage fight. "The children struggled together within her" (Gen. 25:22 ESV). The description in Hebrew reads, "The children smashed themselves inside her."[8] Once, as they kicked at each other, she begged God for an explanation. He gave this:

> "Two nations are in your body,
>> and two groups of people will be taken from
>> you.
> One group will be stronger than the other,
>> and the older will serve the younger."
>
> (GEN. 25:23 NCV)

7

In the ancient clan plan the elder son would inherit superior rank over the younger. Yet in God's plan Jacob would trump Esau. *The older will serve the younger.* Had God not said it, Rebekah never would have imagined it.

> When the time came for her to give birth, there were twin boys in her womb. The first to come out was red, and his whole body was like a hairy garment; so they named him Esau. After this, his brother came out, with his hand grasping Esau's heel; so he was named Jacob. (Gen. 25:24–26 NIV)

Esau grew to look like the guy in charge. Manly, ruddy, and hairy. So hairy that they named him Hairy or, in the mother tongue, Esau, which rhymes with *seesaw,* an apt name for a man whose life was destined to be full of ups and downs.

Esau was a hunter. He had a closet of camo gear and drove a 4x4 truck complete with a rifle rack, mud tires, and a bumper sticker that read "I'd rather be fishing." He was never so happy as when he was tracking a deer or stirring a covey of quail. Bucks. Ducks. Trucks. That was Esau's world. Chuckles loved him.

And Rebekah loved Jacob. He was more metro than macho, more bookish than brawn, more indoor than outdoor, more Saturday in the library than weekend in the wild. Jacob was, well, let me just say it because you'll soon read it. Jacob was a mama's boy. He was a "quiet man and stayed among the tents. Isaac loved Esau. . . . But Rebekah loved Jacob" (Gen. 25:27–28 NCV).

This was some family. Brothers who squared off in the womb. Parents who played favorites. Esau and his brawn, Jacob and his brains. Dysfunction junction. A therapist could have paid her child's college tuition by counseling this brood.

Even so, the twins might have coexisted were it not for the aforementioned birthright privilege. It promised financial perks, preeminence in the clan, twice the inheritance, and all the privileges. But most significant was this: the firstborn of Isaac would be the next bearer of the covenant that God had made with Abraham, namely that God would bless the world through the descendant of Abraham—Jesus Christ (see Gen. 12:3; Acts 3:24–26).[9]

We would logically assume, then, that Jacob would be one special dude, a who's who in the Holy Hall of Holiest People. Shouldn't he love the poor? Comfort the sick? Counsel the distraught? Write proverbs? Pen a few psalms? Be born with an iridescent glow? One would think so.

He did none of the above. He will have his moments. Just not many. He will inspire us, yes. But bewilder us even more. His résumé was more the stuff of the Happy Hour Highball Club than a Sunday school curriculum. He married two sisters but loved only one. He was passive while his wives squabbled. He slept with the maids. His family worshipped foreign gods. He chose to do nothing when his sons went Rambo on a village, slaughtering a tribe. His oldest son had an affair with his maidservant. His favorite son was sold into slavery by his brothers. He spent two decades as a fugitive. He was a dyed-in-the-wool sneak. The guy never preached, prophesied, or said anything worthy of being framed. If you are looking for a star in a Hallmark movie, Jacob is not your guy.

If, on the other hand, you want to see God's steadfast devotion . . .

If you need to know how long God will put up with a scoundrel and his scandals . . .

If you are wondering if God's plan has a place for botchers, bunglers, schemers, and Joad-like last chancers who toss a coin to choose between their will and God's will . . .

If you could benefit from a tale of God's unending, unbending, unswerving faithfulness . . .

If you wonder if God could use a person whose halo has slipped . . .

Then the story of Jacob is what you need.

When God wanted to identify himself to his people, he declared himself to be the God of Abraham, Isaac, and *Jacob.*[10] Not just of Abraham and Isaac. He's also the God of Jacob.

God used Jacob in spite of Jacob. Period.

The word for such devotion? *Grace.* Grace came after Jacob. Grace found him in the desert. Grace protected him when he lived in exile. Grace wrestled him to the ground in Jabbok and blessed him. Grace led him home to Canaan.

Jacob's story is a testimony to divine, unexpected, unrequested, undeserved kindness.

Do you know such grace?

Grace is God as grand marshal, leading his ever-swelling parade of has-beens and never-weres out of halfway houses and prisons and into his palace.

God's grace isn't available just on Sundays. It claims every tick of the clock.

God's grace isn't only as good as you are. God's grace is as good as he is.

God's grace isn't a lucky charm crucifix on a necklace. God's grace is a tiger in your heart.

> God's grace did not happen
> > one time,
> > > long ago.
> God's grace happens
> > now,
> > > today . . . to anyone who'll so much
> > as give God a prayer.

His grace never quits.

That's the kind of God he is—he's the "God of Jacob." Our God is the God of those who struggle and scrape, sometimes barely making it, hanging on for dear life.

So if you are looking for sterling-silver heroes of Scripture, I refer you to Daniel or Joseph. If you are aspiring to split Red Seas or call fire from heaven, Moses and Elijah would be more to your liking.

But if the years have left you cracked in a few places, if the bounce in your step has given way to a limp in your walk, if you wonder, honestly wonder, if you are God's lost cause, then I've got just the story for you.

# CHAPTER 2

# FROM PRINCE TO PALOOKA

Genesis 27:1–28:5

**TO UNDERSTAND THIS CHAPTER'S INTRODUCTION,** you need to hearken back to the days before mobile phones. Yes, there was such an era. In times past—not quite so distant as Noah's, not so recent as today's headlines—there was a segment of history known as the "days of the landline."

Difficult as it may be for millennials and Gen Zers to believe, phones were not always mobile. They did not fit into pockets or purses. They were not wireless or smart. Phones were attached to cables that attached to outlets that attached to telephone lines.

It's true. We walked to school each day in blinding snowstorms with no GPS to guide us or apps to entertain us. Those were primitive times.

The year was 1973. Nixon was president. Watergate was brewing, and I lived in a college dormitory that was, for all practical purposes, cut off from the outside world. We were only allowed to make local calls from our rooms. To speak to someone in another city, we had to use the pay phone.

This wouldn't have been a problem except that I had a crush on a freshman who attended a different college some six hours away. To talk to her I had to pay money. I see the disbelief on your face. Your eyes are widening to the size of quarters, and quarters are exactly what I needed. Many quarters! I had very little money, but I had an idea. The idea is the reason I share this story.

I could charge the cost of the call to someone else. The phone company permitted it. So that's what I did. To whom did I charge the call? My parents? Oh, no, they would never have paid. The girl? No, she was as broke as I was.

I charged the long distance calls to a vacuum cleaner store. It just happened to be a number I found in the phone book. Did I know the store owner? No. Did I ask his permission? No. Did I think I was doing anything dishonest?

That's a good question. Truth is, I wasn't thinking at all. My love-fogged, underdeveloped, barely pubescent, eighteen-year-old brain didn't want to wait until I'd saved enough money. I wanted to get on the phone!

Besides, who would know? *I'm using a pay phone*, I told myself. *How will anyone find out?*

Here's how. The store owner saw the charges and called the phone company. The phone company saw the number I'd dialed and called it. They asked the girl who answered if she knew anyone who might be calling her from a pay phone on the campus of Abilene Christian University.

"Why, yes I do," she said innocently. As far as she knew, I'd won the lottery. As quick as you can say "Max, that was dumb," the dorm director paid me a visit. I, in turn, paid a visit to the office of the dean, wrote an apology to the storeowner and a check to the phone company, and some fifty years later now have used the story to illustrate the stupidity of shortcuts.

That's what I took: a shortcut. Rather than take the honest, responsible, uphill, longer path, I took the wide, downhill, dishonest one.

So did you. And so did every person, other than Jesus, who has taken a breath and taken a step on God's green earth. "All have sinned [*taken shortcuts*] and fall short of the glory of God" (Rom. 3:23 NIV). The bracketed text is my commentary. The scripture just uses the word *sin*. But isn't sin a shortcut?

When Adam and Eve plucked the fruit, they were taking a shortcut. Rather than wait for the Father to fulfill his promises, why not take matters into their own hands?

So they reached for the fruit.

Max reached for the phone.

And you?

"Do I have to answer that?"

Not out loud. But can we agree that all of us at times have chosen the quick and easy route? That sin, at its root, is the unwillingness to wait? To trust? To follow God's plan? We take matters into our own hands.

That's what Jacob did.

Esau, the seesaw, came home from hunting. He had an empty belly. He smelled the pot of red beans that Jacob was stirring over an open fire. The fragrance of simmering onions, garlic, and marbled beef made his mouth water.

"Give me the spoon, Jacob."

The heel-holder sensed an opportunity. "What's it worth to you?"

"Anything. I'm faint with hunger."

"Anything?"

"Name your price. Do you want my bow and arrow? My new knife? Its handle is as long as your foot. It's yours for a bowl of stew."

Maybe at this point Jacob caught a glimpse of his mom giving him the nod. Maybe at this point Jacob caught a vision of the family tree named after him.

"I want the birthright."

"The birthright?"

"Yes, the birthright."

Esau looked at the beans and weighed the options. After a brief thought or two, he sealed his destiny with these words: "What good is a birthright if I'm dead?" (Gen. 25:32 THE MESSAGE).

Esau would not have died. This kerfuffle bore him no threat. He was a hunter; he would have survived. He was big and brawny, twice the brute his baby brother was. He could've coldcocked Jacob with a left hook and finished the soup before Jacob came to his senses.

But instead Esau "shrugged off his rights as the firstborn" (Gen. 25:34 THE MESSAGE). The verb translated as "shrugged off" connotes carelessness or contempt, "despising something as useless."[1] The right of primogeniture was protected by law. A father could not give it to another son (Deut. 21:15–17). The first-born son, however, could forfeit or sell it. This is what Esau did. The birthright was, as far as he could see, an intangible object, invisible, out there somewhere. The beans were right there in front of him. So he agreed to the swap.

"You know what this means, Esau," Jacob explained. "When Dad dies, I get twice what you get."

Esau tied a napkin around his neck. "Twice, yes. Twice."

"It means that I'll be first, not second."

"Whatever you say. Where's the salt?"

"It means that the promise God made to Grandpa Abraham will pass through my side of the family."

"I get it. Now give me a bowl of soup!"

Not to belabor the point, but the burly brother could have so easily picked up his toothpick of a twin and said, "Get out of my way. I'm first in line for everything, including this food!"

But he didn't. He didn't want the entitlement. He let Jacob have it. Years later Jacob would be called Israel, and Israel eventually became the father of the twelve tribes. One of his sons, Judah, fathered a lineage that gave birth to the Lion of Judah, Jesus Christ.

Esau was left with a bowl of beans and a legacy as the one who "for one morsel of food sold his birthright" (Heb. 12:16). Esau took a shortcut.

And Jacob? We cannot let the baby brother get off too easily. Is this the way God's heroes behave? Conniving? Coercing?

Rebekah knew the older would serve the younger.[2] Surely she'd told him. Did God's plan need Jacob's nudge? Of course not. He could have waited for God to act. He *should* have waited. But Rebekah and Jacob took a shortcut.

As we turn the page to Genesis 27, Isaac was on his deathbed. At least he thought he was. The truth is, Isaac was nowhere near death. At 135 years old, he would live another 45 years (Gen. 35:28).[3]

When Isaac was old and his eyes were so weak that he could no longer see, he called for Esau his older son and said to him, "My son."

"Here I am," he answered.

Isaac said, "I am now an old man and don't know the day of my death. Now then, get your equipment—your quiver and bow—and go out to the open country to hunt some wild game for me. Prepare me the kind of tasty food I like and bring it to me to eat, so that I may give you my blessing before I die." (Gen. 27:1–4 NIV)

Rebekah overheard the instructions of Isaac and took Jacob to the side. "Now's our chance," she whispered. She told Jacob to hustle up a hearty meal and take it to Isaac.

Jacob resisted. "Even a cataract-eyed old man can tell us apart." So Rebekah promised to take the blame if the plan failed.

While Esau hunted, Rebekah and Jacob cooked lamb and cut a goatskin. Jacob pulled it over his shoulders and entered his father's tent. Isaac's head trembled under the weight of so many years. Wrinkles cobwebbed his face.

Jacob altered his voice to imitate the husky tone of his brother: "I am Esau, your first son. I have done what you told me. Now sit up and eat some meat of the animal I hunted for you. Then bless me" (Gen. 27:19 NCV).

Isaac fell for the ruse.

"May nations serve you
    and peoples bow down to you.
Be lord over your brothers,
    and may the sons of your mother bow down to you."
(Gen. 27:29 NIV)

Isaac unknowingly crowned the wrong son.

Sometime later big brother, Esau, showed up. As per instructions, he'd prepared a meal for his pop. But his pop was no longer hungry. And the blessing was no longer available. Both Isaac and Esau were dumbfounded.

> Then Isaac trembled exceedingly, and said, ". . . I ate all of it before you came, and I have blessed him—and indeed he shall be blessed."
>
> When Esau heard the words of his father, he cried with an exceedingly great and bitter cry, and said to his father, "Bless me—me also, O my father!"
>
> But [Isaac] said, "Your brother came with deceit and has taken away your blessing."
>
> . . . And Esau said to his father, "Have you only one blessing, my father? Bless me—me also, O my father!" (Gen. 27:33–35, 38)

You and I see an immediate solution to this crisis. Grab Jacob by the nape of the neck and drag him back into the tent where Isaac can *unbless* him and rightly bless Esau. But as odd as it might sound to our Western ears, it just didn't work that way. A blessing had a built-in binding element. It was irreversible and irrevocable. Isaac could give Esau a secondary inheritance, but Jacob had already cashed the check.[4]

I would have expected God to interrupt the story at this point. Like a director unhappy with the actors shouting, "Cut! Cut!," Jacob needed correction. The family needed direction. But God let the deeds unfold.

In case you missed it, let me point something out. Grace just stepped onto the stage. The family is a tinderbox, a spark away from eruption. The brothers bicker. The parents play favorites. Yet God has tethered himself to them.

Grace. The "yet-Godness" of God. We break promises, yet God forgives. We forget commitments, yet God appears. We turn away from him, yet God turns toward us.

That's not to say our waywardness has no consequences. The relationship between the twins crashed like a lawn chair in a tornado. "Esau hated Jacob . . . , and Esau said in his heart, '. . . I will kill my brother'" (Gen. 27:41). Rebekah heard about the pledge from the duped brother, gave Jacob the heads-up, and told him to scoot while the scooting was good. Jacob skedaddled. Rebekah and Jacob got what they wanted, but at what a cost! Sure, Jacob purloined the blessing, but . . .

- his family was splintered,
- he was without a home,
- he had to run for his life,
- his twin wanted to kill him,
- he had betrayed his father's trust,
- and he, as far as we know, never saw his mother again.

He forfeited all the prosperity he would have received from the birthright. No flocks, herds, or possessions. His life was a mare's nest of misery. The next time we see him he'll use a rock for a pillow. Jacob went from prince to palooka in a day.

All because he took a shortcut.

All because he couldn't wait.

And us? What shortcuts are we taking in life? God has promised to give us all that we need. A garden of Eden of joy, hope, life, and love is ours for the asking. All we need to do is wait on God. But he is so slow! His timing is out of sync with ours.

So we cut corners. We cheat, if not the owner of the vacuum cleaner store, we cheat on exams, on taxes. We deceive. Not with goatskins and a lamb, but with lies, exaggerations, and misstatements. We polish apples, inflate facts, drop names, and work the system.

> "God wants me to have this job. I'll just pad my résumé."
> "God wants me to be happy. I've found happiness in the arms of a woman who is not my wife."
> "I know God wants me to tell the truth. But in this case the truth will get me into trouble. A little lie won't hurt."

How many shortcuts have been justified with the best of intentions?

At the sentencing for her role in the 2019 college admissions bribery scandal, actress Lori Loughlin addressed the court:

> "I made an awful decision. I went along with a plan to give my daughters an unfair advantage in the college admissions process. In doing so, I ignored my intuition and allowed myself to be swayed from my moral compass.
>
> "I thought I was acting out of love for my children, but in reality it only undermined and diminished my daughters' abilities and accomplishments."[5]

A wrong shortcut, even one taken for the right reasons, always causes someone pain. It is a labyrinth honeycombed with trip wires.

There are no shortcuts with God. None. Zilch. Zero. He doesn't need your foot on his accelerator. He doesn't need my help with his plans. If God had wanted Jacob to have the blessing, Jacob would have had the blessing. Rebekah didn't need to connive. Jacob didn't need to deceive. If God wanted Jacob to carry the mantle, it was as good as done.

All Rebekah and Jacob needed to do was the one thing they found hard to do: wait on the Lord.

How about you?

What are you seeking? Needing? Wanting?

A spouse? Wait on the Lord.

A new job? Wait on the Lord.

Your husband to come home? Your ship to come in? Your career to look up? Your business to take off? If so, here is what you need to know. God's timing is always right. His plan is always best. His will never includes deception or manipulation. His strategy never destroys people or requires compromise. He never badgers, battles, belittles, or bruises people. If you are doing so, then you are not in God's will. You may think he is slow to act, but he is not. Trust him . . . and wait.

Keep your head up, knees bent, eyes clear. Wait on the Lord. Take the narrow road and the uphill path. Be the employee who does the work, the student who studies for the test.

And pay for your own phone calls. If you can't pay the charge, just stay in your room, do your homework, and stay out of trouble.

You never know. You might meet the girl of your dreams right there on campus. I did. I was a few short semesters away from meeting the love of my life. True love, as it turned out, was a local call away.

CHAPTER 3

# LADDERS FROM HEAVEN

Genesis 28:10–17

**YOU'VE HAD, OR WILL HAVE, MOMENTS OF DEEP** despair. You've had, or will have, hours in which your eyes weep a river, and your heart breaks into a thousand pieces. You've had, or will have, journeys through dry, barren stretches that will leave you exhausted and isolated.

You will feel stripped of all you cherish. You will look around and see no one to comfort you. You will search for strength, but you will search in vain, for strength will not come.

Yet in that desolate moment as you sit near the headstone and cry, on the barstool and drink, or in your bedroom and sigh, God will meet you. You will sense and see him as never before.

Do not begrudge the barren stretches, for in the barrenness we encounter God. We find the presence of God. Jacob did. And no one was more surprised than he.

In one fell swoop he'd tricked his brother and aging father. Rebekah, the mom of the twins, saw Esau's rage and raced to warn Jacob. "He's got that look in his eyes. Don't pack a bag. Don't grab a cloak. Don't stop running and don't look back." Seesaw was on Heel's heels. She told him to hightail it to the land of her brother Laban and to stay there while Esau cooled down.

Jacob did exactly that. He grabbed a waterskin and filled a sack with figs and fruit and, with one final glance at his mother, mounted a camel and left. He set out from Beersheba to go to Mesopotamia (modern-day Turkey): 550 miles.[1]

Life was in free fall. Jacob left behind a weeping mother, a seething brother, and an aging, angry father. He had no herds. No servants to serve him. No guards to protect him. No cooks to prepare food for him. No companions. No resources.

Nada.

Jacob was raised in Fortune 500 wealth, surrounded by servants, shepherds, and slaves. His grandfather was "rich in livestock, in silver, and in gold" (Gen. 13:2). Abraham and his nephew Lot were so blessed that "the land was not able to support them . . . their possessions were so great that they could not dwell together" (Gen. 13:6). This affluence was passed down to Abraham's son. "[Isaac] began to prosper, and continued prospering until he became very prosperous; for he had possessions of flocks and possessions of herds and a great number of servants" (Gen. 26:13–14).

Jacob was the grandson of a baron. The son of an aristocrat. Had he lived today, he would have been raised in a mansion, pampered by servants, and educated in the finest schools. He had everything he needed. And then, from one moment to the next, he had nothing. He ran for his life, suddenly and utterly alone.

In the first two days he traveled forty-three miles from Beersheba to Bethel, a barren moorland that lay about eleven miles north of Jerusalem.[2] The land through which he hiked was scorched and strewn with rocks, bleak like wasteland.

On the evening of the second day, as the sun set over a village called Luz, he stopped for the night. He did not enter the city. Perhaps its occupants were dangerous people. Perhaps Jacob was insecure. Why he stopped short of Luz is not revealed. What we are told is this: "He took one of the stones of that place and put it at his head, and he lay down in that place to sleep" (Gen. 28:11).

Without so much as a bedroll for his head, he was the Bronze Age version of the prodigal son. The desert was his pigpen. But the prodigal in the parable did something Jacob did not do. "[He] came to himself" (Luke 15:17). He snapped to his senses. He looked at the pigs he was feeding, considered the life he was leading, and determined, "I will arise and go to my father" (Luke 15:18).

Jacob showed no such initiative. He made no resolve, displayed no conviction of sin, showed no remorse. Jacob did not pray, as did Jonah, or weep, as did Peter. In fact, Jacob's lack of repentance is what makes the next scene one of the great stories of grace in the Bible.

Daylight dulled to gold. The sun slid low like a half-lidded eye. Orange gave way to ebony. Stars began to flicker. Jacob dozed, and in a dream he saw:

A ladder resting on the earth and reaching up into heaven, and he saw angels of God going up and coming down the ladder. Then Jacob saw the LORD standing above the ladder. (Gen. 28:12–13 NCV)

A ziggurat spanned the distance between Jacob's barren, borrowed bed of dirt and heaven's highest, holiest dwelling. The stairway was aflurry with activity: angels ascending, angels descending. Their moving was a rush of lights, back and forth, up and down. The Hebrew wording of Jacob's response implies raised arms and open mouth. A direct translation would be "There, a ladder! Oh, angels! And look, *the Lord himself*!" (v. 16, emphasis added).[3]

When Jacob awoke, he realized that he was not alone. He'd felt alone. He'd assumed he was alone. He appeared to be alone. But he was surrounded by august citizens of heaven!

So are we.

Millions of mighty spiritual beings walk on earth around us. More than eighty thousand angels stood ready to come to the aid of Christ.[4] Scripture speaks of "countless thousands of angels in a joyful gathering" (Heb. 12:22 NLT). When John, the apostle, caught a glimpse of heaven, he saw "ten thousand times ten thousand, and thousands of thousands" (Rev. 5:11). Can you do the math on that statement? Nor can I. Angels are to heaven what stars are to the night sky. Too many to count!

What is their task? "All the angels are spirits who serve God and are sent to help those who will receive salvation" (Heb. 1:14 NCV). There is never an airplane on which you travel or a classroom into which you enter that you are not preceded and surrounded by God's mighty servants. "He has put his angels in charge of you to watch over you wherever you go" (Ps. 91:11 NCV).

Sheila Walsh experienced the promise of the passage. At the age of thirty-four she admitted herself into a psychiatric hospital. One would not have suspected any cause for concern. Just the day prior she had cohosted a well-watched national television broadcast. Yet a storm raged within.

Eventually Sheila would be diagnosed as a victim of depression and PTSD. But on the first night no one knew what was wrong. The hospital staff placed her on suicide watch. Sheila had every reason to feel all alone. But she wasn't.

In the early-morning hours of day two, Sheila noticed that another person had entered her room. She had been sitting for hours with her head buried in her lap. Upon sensing the presence of the visitor, she lifted her gaze. The visitor was part of the suicide watch, she assumed. But something was different. He was a strong man with tender eyes. As her mind tried to process who he might be, the man placed something in her hands—a small stuffed toy: a lamb. He told her, "Sheila, the Shepherd knows where to find you." And with that her guest was gone.

God had sent an angel to her.

Around six that morning Sheila awoke to the sound of orderlies entering her room. She had fallen asleep on the floor. There at the foot of her folding chair was the lamb the man had delivered hours before.[5]

Jacob was not given a lamb, but he was given heaven's comfort. The message of the vision could not be clearer: when we are at our lowest, God is watching over us from the highest. Between us stretches a conduit of grace upon which messengers carry out his will.

These angels convey our prayers into God's presence. In the apostle John's vision, he saw an "Angel, carrying a gold censer, [who] came and stood at the Altar. He was given a great quantity of incense so that he could offer up the prayers of all the holy people of God on the Golden Altar before the Throne" (Rev. 8:3–4 THE MESSAGE).

As God hears our petitions, he responds with thunder! "Then the Angel filled the censer with fire from the Altar and heaved it to earth. It set off thunders, voices, lightnings, and an earthquake" (Rev. 8:5 THE MESSAGE).

Our prayers have a thermostatic impact upon the actions of heaven.

Mothers, when you pray for your child . . .

Husbands, when you ask for healing in your marriage . . .

Children, when you kneel at your bed before going to sleep . . .

Citizens, when you pray for your country . . .

Pastors, when you pray for the members of your church . . .

Your prayers trigger the ascension of angels and the downpour of power!

Jacob saw heavenly activity. One might well wonder why God would pull back the veil and show Jacob the hosts that surrounded him. After all, Jacob had not sought God. Yet what Jacob saw scarcely compares with what Jacob heard. You'd expect a lecture, a holy scolding. But God gave Jacob something altogether different. God told Jacob that he would make him and his descendants a great people who would cover the earth. Despite Jacob's deception and shortcuts, God repeated to him the blessing he gave Abraham and Isaac: "I am with you and will watch over you wherever you go, and I will bring you back to this land. I will not leave you" (Gen. 28:15 NIV). The fugitive had not been abandoned. The trickster had not been cast aside. God committed himself to the lifelong care of Jacob.

Again we might wonder why. Had Jacob done anything to show he was worthy of the blessing? No. Jacob had done nothing but slimy stuff thus far. He leaked integrity like a sieve. He played his brother like a two-dollar fiddle. He worked the system like a riverboat gambler. There is, thus far, not one mention of Jacob in prayer, Jacob in faith, or Jacob in earnest pursuit of God.

Even so, God drenched his undeserving fugitive with a Niagara of unexpected kindness.

God did not turn away from one who had turned away from him. He was faithful. He still is. "If we are faithless, he remains faithful" (2 Tim. 2:13 NIV).

Just ask my friend William. He had everything going for him. He'd been raised in a supportive home by terrific parents. He played on the golf team of the prestigious Wake Forest University. He was bright enough to be fast-tracked on an MBA program.

But he drank too much. He experimented with drugs and violated team rules. His scholarship was in jeopardy. His future was in question. William was despondent. He was on the verge of losing it all when God spoke to him. (William paused as he told me this story. "I'm not flaky, Max. I was raised Presbyterian. Our idea of being charismatic is to lift one finger off our lap.")

Yet God spoke to him in a manner every bit as vivid as the way God spoke to Jacob. William was alone on a dirt path in the woods when he saw Jesus. "Everything you've been told about me is true," the Savior said. "I am here. I love you. It's time for you to come home."

William did. He changed peer groups and found a spiritual mentor. He eventually changed his major from business to theology. He went on to serve for decades as a minister and now directs a job placement organization that serves churches and nonprofits worldwide.

What God did for Jacob, God did for William. God sought him and called him.

He did the same for Matthew. I share his story with his permission but without using his real name. His struggle involves pornography, and he doesn't want to risk embarrassing his family.

Yet he is eager to brag on God's goodness. Pornography had Matthew by the collar—internet, magazines, adult shops. The gravitational pull was a lure Matthew could not shake.

His Jacob's ladder moment occurred as he walked down a busy city street, having just spent the afternoon in a seedy strip club. The remorse of his fall, yet another fall, fell on him like a net on a prey. "Lord, I don't deserve grace yet another time," he mumbled.

God spoke into his thoughts. "Of course you don't. That's why I call it grace. My child, you are forgiven. I forgave you the first time you ever requested. I'll forgive you the final time."

At that moment Matthew said he came to understand the scripture "God's kindness is meant to lead you to repentance" (Rom. 2:4 ESV). Matthew experienced a new beginning.

Grace does this. It pursues. Persists. Shows up and speaks up. In our dreams. In our despair. In our guilt. Grace is God on the move saying, "I am with you and will watch over you wherever you go. . . . I will not leave you until I have done what I have promised you" (Gen. 28:15 NIV).

Extraordinary, don't you think? Jacob certainly felt so. "Then Jacob awoke from his sleep and said, 'Surely the LORD is in this place, and I did not know it'" (Gen. 28:16).

How many people could say the same? The Lord is in this place, but they don't know it. They are unacquainted with the God who meets us. They believe in a God who created the world but not a God who is involved in the world. A God who made the universe but not a God who makes a difference in the day-to-day. A God who started it all, but not a God who walks in the midst of it all. Christian atheists, they are.

Their faith has a limp because they do not recognize the presence of God.

God was—is!—speaking to you. Inviting you to look up to him, lean into him. That is him! Standing at the top of the ladder. Sending angels to help you, receiving the angels who deliver your prayers.

Don't believe me? You think the invitation was limited to a patriarch in the desert of Beersheba? Then hasten to the Gospel of John and hear what Jesus says to you and me: "Truly, truly, I say to you, you will see heaven opened, and the angels of God ascending and descending on the Son of Man" (John 1:51 ESV). Your ladder into heaven is not a vision. Yours is a person. Jesus is our stairway.

He calls himself the "Son of Man," a title that refers to his preexistence. It is used eighty-two times in the Gospels and eighty-one of those occasions were by Jesus himself.[6] He is, in essence, announcing, "I am the one upon whom the angels ascend and descend. I am the vehicle of blessing to the world."

Christ, our go-between, is everywhere at all times, equally present with the Father to hear our prayers as he is with the Spirit to answer them. "There is one God and one mediator so that human beings can reach God. That way is through Christ Jesus" (1 Tim. 2:5 NCV). He is at both ends of the ladder: Jehovah at the top, Jehovah at the bottom.

He is the conduit through which blessings come and prayers

ascend. He is the intermediary between you and God. The question is not "Is he active?" The question is "Are we watching?"

Jacob was away from his family, an escapee from his brother, a victim of his own folly. The vulture pecking at his joy was reared in its own nest. He was penniless and homeless, not even a blanket for his head. He thought he'd lost it all, but in actuality he'd found it all. He found a heavenly Father who found him first.

Jacob responded admirably. "He took the stone he had used for his pillow and stood it up as a memorial pillar and poured oil over it. He christened the place Bethel (God's House)" (Gen. 28:18–19 THE MESSAGE).

Jacob turned his pillow into a pillar and renamed the place of his pain. The stone pillow, a symbol of all he lacked, became a holy pillar, a memorial to all he found. The land was a windswept badland no longer. It was a place of God.

What is your version of a stone pillow? What reminds you of mistakes you've made, things you've lost? A divorce decree? A headstone? The picture of the kids who forgot you?

What is your version of a desert? An empty house? A hospital room? A desktop of unpaid bills?

The promise of Jacob and Bethel is this: the Lord is in the wilderness, in the despair, in the misery, mess, and mayhem, and in broken hearts. God will meet you in this unwanted and unwelcome waypoint. With his help your pillow will become a pillar; your barren land will become a place of worship. God will speak, angels will come, and you will soon declare: "The LORD is in this place, and I did not know it."

CHAPTER 4

# NO QUID PRO QUO

Genesis 28:20–22

**GOD HAD NOT DONE HIS PART. IT BOILED DOWN** to that. He had not kept his end of the deal.

And I was upset. I'd done what I'd said I'd do.

But God? Heaven could not make the same claim.

So it was time for a reckoning, a comeuppance. The hour had arrived for me to air my complaint. I did exactly that. On a cold December night in 1985, I drove to the vast West Texas prairie and parked my father's Chevrolet sedan next to a pumpjack. I did not live in Texas at the time. I lived in Rio de Janeiro, Brazil. I'd been raised in Texas, however. My father had made a career in the oil fields. He and Brazil were the subjects of my agreement with God.

I would go to Brazil, and, in turn, God would heal my father.

Simple as that. Dad was diagnosed with ALS in 1982. Denalyn and I were planning to move to Rio in 1983. Upon his diagnosis we offered to abandon our plans and stay close to him. He would hear none of it. In a letter that I treasure, he told us, "I have no fear of death or eternity. Just go and please God."

Before we went, God and I reached an understanding. We would forgo precious days with Dad, and, in exchange, God would do what doctors could not do: heal my father. The result would be a marquee testimony: "God heals father of sacrificial missionary." Dad would enjoy restored health. The church would have a story to tell for decades to come. What a win-win for the kingdom!

There was just one problem. Dad's condition did not improve. It worsened. We were called back to Texas on emergency leave. We rushed to the hospital to find him intubated and weak. I spent the day in the ICU waiting room, churning on the inside.

That night I went to the oil field, stomped back and forth on the flat, graveled ground, and filed my grievances.

"Did I not go to Brazil?"

Silence.

"Did I not relocate my family?"

Silence.

"Did I not do what I said I would do?"

Silence.

"Then why won't you heal my father?"

Silence.

God did not speak. And even then I knew why. The arrangement was a figment of my imagination. It bore only one signature. And it revealed a misunderstanding I had about God.

Jacob suffered from the same misconception.

When we last left him, Jacob was wide-eyed from a most mystical moment. He saw the unseen. He was privileged a peek at the sacred portal between the realms. Stone steps connected heaven with earth. Angels ascended and descended upon them. God, from above, spoke words of affirmation to Jacob down below: every blessing enjoyed by Abraham and Isaac would be continued in the life of Jacob.

Jacob's theophany left him with an epiphany: "God has been in this place." Terror and adoration were rightly mixed. He turned his pillow into a pillar, anointed it with oil, and called the barren stretch of land "the house of God."

We expect that this encounter would leave him a changed man, aware of his shortcomings. That was certainly the case for other people in Scripture who had a bare-faced rendezvous with the Almighty.

God spoke to Isaiah in a vision similar to Jacob's. The moment prompted Isaiah to cry out, "Woe is me, for I am undone! Because I am a man of unclean lips" (Isa. 6:5).

When Peter witnessed Christ performing a miracle on the Sea of Galilee, he realized the divinity of Jesus. He fell at Jesus' feet and declared: "Depart from me, for I am a sinful man, O Lord!" (Luke 5:8).

The curtain of heaven was pulled back enough for John to witness twenty-four elders and four living creatures worshipping God. The apostle was so overcome he turned to the angel and "fell at his feet to worship him. But [the angel] said to me, '. . . do not do that! . . . Worship God!'" (Rev. 19:10).

Isaiah was undone. Peter was overwhelmed. John worshipped.

We expect something similar from Jacob. But, alas, any awe he might have felt quickly evaporated, and he began to negotiate with God.

> Then Jacob made a vow, saying, "If God will be with me and will watch over me on this journey I am taking and will give me food to eat and clothes to wear so that I return safely to my father's household, then the LORD will be my God and this stone that I have set up as a pillar will be God's house, and of all that you give me I will give you a tenth." (Gen. 28:20–22 NIV)

Do you see the language of mediation? "If you will . . . then I will . . ."

If you, God, will . . .

> be with me,
> watch over me,
> feed me,
> clothe me,
> return me to my father's household,

> then I, Jacob, will . . .

> declare you as my God,
> build you a house of worship,
> give you one-tenth of all you give me.

Jacob haggled. Rather than receive the blessing and be grateful, the bargain hunter hammered out the key points of a contract.

He spoke to God the way he would speak to a camel trader. He suggested a contract. A transaction. An agreement.

Others did something similar. Abraham begged God to withhold his wrath on Sodom if there were ten righteous people (Gen. 18:32). Hannah pledged to consecrate her child if God would give her one (1 Sam. 1:11). No, Jacob wasn't the first to negotiate with God. Yet he went further than Abraham and Hannah. His belief in God was contingent upon God's protection of him. *Feed me, oversee me,* then *I will declare you as my God.*

A few days ago I met with a young couple. Their toddler was injured in a car accident. When I visited them in the hospital, the child was on life support. As we stood outside the ICU and spoke, I saw, not sorrow in their eyes, but anger. Anger at God.

"If he takes my son," growled the young father, "I will never believe in him again."

The wife nodded with pursed lips and clinched fists.

Who can fault their sorrow? Yet who are we to make such a declaration? Dare we hinge our belief on God's response to our prayers?

A working term for this might be *transactional theology.* Transactional theology presupposes that we meet God on equal terms. *He's got what I want. I have what he wants.* So we reach an agreement.

"If you heal my father, I'll move to Rio."

"If you help me in this interview, I'll be kind to my husband."

"If you get me out of prison, I'll be a preacher."

"If you do this, I'll do that."

Really? On what basis do we negotiate with God?

A. W. Tozer wrote, "Left to ourselves we tend immediately

43

to reduce God to manageable terms. We want to get Him where we can use Him, or at least know where He is when we need Him. We want a God we can in some measure control."[1]

Anytime we suggest that we control spiritual dividends from God, that God is a genie who awaits our rub on the lamp, that God is an ATM who dispenses goodness if we enter the correct PIN, that God is a sky fairy who is under obligation to do what we want because we have thrashed out a deal with him, we border on heresy. We've exchanged a transcendent God to whom we're accountable for a dependent God who's accountable to us.

The result of a transactional faith?

Disillusionment. How many times have you heard someone say something like "I gave up on God years ago. My child was sick. I said, 'God if you are up there, please heal my child.' No healing. So as far as I'm concerned, no God."

How many people have found themselves in their version of a West Texas oil field, looking into an inky night sky and demanding, "Why don't you do your part?" How many people have reduced God to a pocket-sized deity? How many people have missed out on a vibrant, life-giving relationship with our great Father because their view of him is small and their view of self is inflated?

Let it be stated clearly and understood deeply: there is no quid pro quo with God. He is not a flea market peddler. There is no tit for tat, this for that, our part for God's part.

Scripture counters transactional theology with this message: God likes us, but he is not like us. Jesus taught us to pray: "Our Father in heaven, hallowed be Your name" (Matt. 6:9). The root word for *hallowed* is *hagios* from which we derive the words *holy* and *holiness*. It carries with it the meaning of "unique, different, separated."[2] Again, God likes you. But he is not like you.

> Gravity does not pull him.
> Pain does not plague him.
> The economy does not faze him.
> The weather does not disturb him.
> Elections do not define him.
> Diseases do not infect him.
> Death cannot claim him.

He is above all this!

He is "the Most High over all the earth" (Ps. 83:18 ESV). The earth is his footstool (see Isa. 66:1). Our world fits in his pocket. Our universe could sit in his palm. He is holy. He fills heaven and earth as the ocean fills the bucket that is submerged in it. God is not contained. He contains.

God is to us what my brother and I were to our ant farm. My brother built it as a middle school science project. It was a simple device: two clear panes of plastic separated by an inch of dirt. The panels were a square foot in size, and the dirt was populated by ants. They were busy little creatures: burrowing tunnels, scurrying through their labyrinth of chambers and caverns.

Though we could see everything about their existence, they were oblivious to ours. As far as they knew, the entire universe consisted of a square foot of dirt.

What was easy for me was impossible for them. I could ride my bike down the block. I could toss a baseball with my buddies.

I was only a fourth grader, but in comparison with the ants, I was "the most high."

Imagine my surprise when one of the ants attempted to strike a deal with me.

One evening as I was finishing fourth-grade homework, I heard a high-pitched and squeaky voice.

"Max!"

I looked away from my textbook and saw the tiniest of bugs standing on an even tinier clod of dirt.

"Max," he repeated, "I want to make a swap with you!"

I glanced around to make certain my brother wasn't playing a trick. He wasn't. This was a legitimate shout-out from an ant farm dweller.

"What do you mean?" I answered.

"I want to be promoted to the king of the ant hill. You make that happen for me, and I'll give you this piece of dirt."

He pointed to the fleck on which he was standing.

"I don't want your dirt," I told him.

"I'll give you a bread crumb," he countered.

"I don't want your bread crumb," I replied. "Besides, I gave you the crumb to begin with."

This went on for several minutes. He even promised me a vacation in his two-bedroom ant-tunnel condo. Finally I told him to quit bugging me. "You don't get it. You have nothing that I need. I have everything you need. Your farm exists because I wanted it to exist."

He walked away in a huff. "I don't believe in Max anymore!"

He became an *antheist.*

All right, the story is a bit overstated. But the point of it is not.

God, to an infinitely greater degree, is "higher" than we are. Our planet is but an ant farm to him. The depths of the earth are nothing but wrinkles in God's hand. The highest mountain is smaller than his smallest toe. "He is not interchangeable with any creature in heaven or on earth, or with the likeness of any product of human imagination. He is sovereign, and His name is holy above every other name, and not to be named with any other in the same breath."[3]

Nothing stunts spiritual development more than a flea market view of God. If you and I think he is puny enough to need our help, we'll soon abandon our pursuit of him. If, on the other hand, we see God as he truly is, holy and high apart, transcendent and resplendent, then we will spend a lifetime doing what we will do for eternity—exploring the beauty and riches of our heavenly Father.

> Here's the reality: most people who are angry with God are angry with him for being God. They're not angry because he has failed to deliver what *he* promised. They're angry because he has failed to deliver what *they* have craved, expected, or demanded. When awe of self replaces awe of God, God ceases to be your Lord and is reduced to being your indentured servant.[4]

God does not exist for us. We exist for God! God does not exist to make a big deal out of Max. Max exists to make a big deal out of God.

With that in mind, can we appreciate the folly in thinking we have anything to offer God that he does not have?

And can we applaud the stunning, surprising patience of God?

Jacob thought his allegiance was so valuable that God would meet his terms in order to receive it. I thought my service as a missionary was strategic enough to exchange for a supernatural healing.

Monstrous self-exaltation.

Yet God responded with grace. A grace described by the psalmist:

> The LORD is compassionate and gracious,
>> slow to anger, abounding in love.
> He will not always accuse,
>> nor will he harbor his anger forever;
> he does not treat us as our sins deserve
>> or repay us according to our iniquities.
> For as high as the heavens are above the earth,
>> so great is his love for those who fear him;
> as far as the east is from the west,
>> so far has he removed our transgressions from us.
> As a father has compassion on his children,
>> so the LORD has compassion on those who
>>> fear him;
> for he knows how we are formed,
>> he remembers that we are dust. (Ps. 103:8–14 NIV)

To be clear, God hears our prayers. He is not put off by our pleas. I was right to pray for my dad. You are obedient when you ask for help. But please be careful. Prayer is not asking God to do what you want; it is trusting God to do what is best. God loves us so much he took on human form and became one of us. He took on feet, hands, and eyes. He even allowed himself to be killed by his creation. He is not turned away by our requests. But he will not be reduced to a God of quid pro quo.

He is too large.

We are too small.

By the way, God did heal my dad, not on this planet, but in his presence. And I'm sure my father would be the first to say that he received the best possible answer to his son's prayer.

# CHAPTER 5

# THE TRICKSTER GETS TRICKED

---

Genesis 29

I'VE HAD A FEW ARGUMENTS WITH SCALES. NOT fish scales. Weight scales. I've stared at the number and refuted, "No, you can't be correct. You're inaccurate. You're overweighing me. I'm not that heavy! You're wrong."

But the scales never reply. They remain mute. They do not defend themselves. It does no good to contend with scales about your weight.

It does no good to argue with the mirror about your appearance. Even so, I did. Denalyn commented on my bald spot. I didn't know I had one. Apparently it was spreading on my scalp years before I noticed it. Thanks to my dear, observant wife, I'm ignorant no longer. I hurried to the bathroom and held a hand mirror so I could see the back of my head. There it was. Sitting like a yarmulke, spreading like an amoeba. You've seen the monks who shave a saucer-sized circle on their heads?

I qualify.

I expressed my displeasure to the mirrors. "You must be incorrect." No reply. They, like the bathroom scales, are impervious to objections.

So is the radar gun. "That can't be true, officer. I wasn't speeding."

"The radar gun says otherwise."

Growl. Case closed. No rebuttal allowed.

It's hard to deny the truth when it stares at you squarely in the face.

In Jacob's case God gave him a face full of facts in the distant land of Haran. You'll find his twenty-year sojourn there one of the most curious, entertaining, and fascinating stories in the Bible. Can a man marry one woman all the while thinking he is marrying someone else? Would a swindler ever be outswindled by another swindler? Genesis 29 offers answers.

Before we follow Jacob to Haran, keep in mind that Jacob was a player in heaven's greatest promise: the deliverance of Jesus to earth. Two generations earlier God had spoken to Abraham, Jacob's grandfather, and promised, in so many words, "I'm going to do something about the misery, death, and brokenness in the world. And I'm going to do it through you and your descendants."

One of those descendants was Jacob. From the top of Jacob's ladder God promised, "in your seed all the families of the earth shall be blessed" (Gen. 28:14). Yet, Jacob's rap sheet included words like *cheater, deceiver, trickster, grifter,* and *liar.* His spiritual life had more ups and downs than the Rocky Mountains.

But God kept him on the team. God used the man in spite of the man. Odd, I know. Jacob seemed more at home in a gambling casino than in a church sanctuary. He was a bit of a mess, this guy.

Aren't we all? Like him, our spiritual walk follows a crooked path. Our cheese keeps falling off our cracker, and our bad habits scuttle our good intentions. And we wonder, does God have a place for us?

The answer through Jacob is "yes." Our failures are great, but God's grace is greater. He uses flawed folks. He doesn't cast us out when we deserve it. He does, however, let us reap what we sow.

Scripture waves this warning flag often and with no small amount of flair.

"The wicked are trapped by their own deeds." (Ps. 9:16 NLT)

"Cruel people bring trouble on themselves." (Prov. 11:17 NCV)

"The unfaithful are destroyed by their duplicity." (Prov. 11:3 NIV)

"The wicked are brought down by their own wickedness." (Prov. 11:5 NIV)

"As you have done, it will be done to you;
     your deeds will return upon your own head."
          (Obad. 1:15 NIV)

"The nations have fallen into the pit they dug.
     Their feet are caught in the nets they laid." (Ps. 9:15 NCV)

The list of such advisements goes on and on.[1] The fact that we reap what we sow is no small matter in Scripture. Evil rebounds.

So does good.

"Forgive, and you will be forgiven." (Luke 6:37 NCV)

> "Well-spoken words bring satisfaction;
> well-done work has its own reward."
> (Prov. 12:14 THE MESSAGE)

> "Kind people do themselves a favor,
> but cruel people bring trouble on themselves."
> (Prov. 11:17 NCV)

> "Whoever gives to others will get richer;
> those who help others will themselves be
> helped." (Prov. 11:25 NCV)

Jesus summed up the bounce-back principle when he said, "With the measure you use, it will be measured to you" (Matt. 7:2 NIV).

Do you want God to disperse mercy upon you with a bucket? Then use a bucket as you disperse mercy to others. Would you want him to use a teaspoon? Then . . . well, you get the point.

I'm not sure Jacob did.

To help him learn it, God took Jacob to the land of Laban, the region known as Haran.

Rebekah, his mother, commissioned this journey. Her plan

was simple: send Jacob to a safe place where he could stay with her brother Laban while Esau's anger subsided. Who knows, while there he might find a nice young girl to marry.

Jacob thought he was going to Haran to meet his uncle and marry a wife. God, however, sent Jacob to Haran so Jacob could step on the scales. It was time to look in the mirror. It was time to read the radar gun. It was time for Jacob to face the facts about Jacob. He had, not a bald spot, but a few blind spots. He traveled east across the Jordan River, north toward Damascus, east to Tadmor, then a sharp north over the Euphrates River and through the Fertile Crescent into modern-day Turkey.

The first thing Jacob saw in Haran was a water well. A stone plugged the mouth to prevent pollution and theft. Three shepherds stood near the well. Jacob asked if they knew a man named Laban. They said they did.

> While he was still talking with them, Rachel came with her father's sheep, for she was a shepherd. When Jacob saw Rachel daughter of his uncle Laban, and Laban's sheep, he went over and rolled the stone away from the mouth of the well and watered his uncle's sheep. Then Jacob kissed Rachel and began to weep aloud. (Gen. 29:9–11 NIV)

What a made-for-movie moment! I see Rachel with dark hair that was gathered at the nape of her neck by a scarlet string. Her eyes were the color of chocolate and shaped like almonds. Her chin had a slight cleft. Her mouth, a shy smile. She shepherded her flock with a willow branch.

She was a portrait of charm, this Rachel.

She walks in beauty, like the night
Of cloudless climes and starry skies;
And all that's best of dark and bright
Meet in her aspect and her eyes.[2]

She was a knockout. And Jacob fell head over heels.

One sight of her and he ripped open his robe, revealing the *S* on his chest. Pop-eyed and palpitating, he flexed his pecs, pressed his shoulder against the stone, and gave it a heave. The rock gave way. Jacob did what the three men had yet to do. He then did what no one imagined he would do. "He kissed Rachel and broke into tears" (Gen. 29:11 THE MESSAGE).

Commentaries describe this kiss as a respected and expected cultural gesture.[3] A slight peck on the cheek. Really?

I see passion. I see Jacob cupping her face in his hands and kissing her like it was their wedding day. He then wept. For her beauty? For the end of his pilgrimage? At the thought that he, the heel grabber, would meet such a queen? Maybe all of the above.

The name Rachel means "ewe" (as in lamb).[4] The moment Jacob saw her, he said, "I want ewe." (Sorry, couldn't resist.) Rachel ran and fetched her father, Laban.

Prepare yourself for this guy. He was a slick one. Part Bernie Madoff, part P. T. Barnum. Ponzi meister and circus promoter. He could, at once, put an arm around your shoulders and his hand on your wallet. He wore his silk shirt unbuttoned to the navel, a gold chain around his neck, and gold rings on each pinkie. His hair was colored with grocery store hair dye that didn't match his sideburns.

He gave Jacob a squeeze.

"Oh, Rebekah's boy! You will come to my tent. You will live in my house! You will want for nothing as long as you are here."

Jacob went to work for Laban and, after a month of tending his flocks, requested permission to marry Rachel. The typical bride price was thirty to forty shekels. Since a shepherd's annual wage was ten shekels a year, Jacob most likely expected to work three or four years for the hand of Rachel.[5] Boy, was he in for a surprise.

I imagine the conversation went something like this:

"What would you take in exchange for the hand of your
    daughter?"
Laban placed a hand over his heart. "I could never give up
    my precious Rachel."
"I'll work for you."
"I could never accept labor from my sister's son."
"I'll tend your flocks for a year."
"But Rachel is my special daughter."
"I'll serve for three years."
"But Rachel has such beauty."

Jacob, who'd moved the stone to impress Rachel, was willing to move heaven and earth to marry her. "Four years."

Back and forth they volleyed until Jacob agreed to work seven years (double the expected dowry!) for only room and board.

Remember, this was Jacob, the grandson of the richest man in the promised land. And he was working for free? Either Rachel was drop-dead gorgeous, or greedy Laban could talk birds out of trees. I suspect that both were the case.

Some of the Bible's most poetic language was used to describe the romance between Jacob and Rachel. "So Jacob served seven years for Rachel, and they seemed only a few days to him because of the love he had for her" (Gen. 29:20).

*Sigh.*

All would have gone well had Laban not been such a backroom dealer. Rachel had an older sister named Leah, who was still single. Scripture is a bit cryptic about her appearance: "Leah's eyes were delicate, but Rachel was beautiful of form and appearance" (Gen. 29:17). *Delicate* means "soft." Leah's eyes lacked the fire and sparkle of her younger sister's. Whereas the name Rachel meant "ewe," the name Leah meant "cow."[6]

"Ewe" and "moo" in the same family.

A reflection on her appearance? Seems to be the case. "While Leah is not without striking features, she pales in comparison to Rachel's overall beauty."[7] What we can say with certainty is that Rachel was heading to the wedding altar, and her big sister, Leah, was not. Laban, however, had other plans. I do not know how to say "switcheroo" in Hebrew, but Laban pulled off the biggest one in the Bible.

The day of the wedding finally arrived; seven years of labor were completed. Laban invited everyone. The brickmakers, the goatherds, and shepherds. The grain-growing farmers and the camel-riding merchants. "Laban gathered together all the men of the place and made a feast" (Gen. 29:22). The word for *feast* means "drinking fest."[8] Wine flowed like water. Everyone drank and danced. There was hand clapping, music making, joke telling, backslapping, drumbeating, meat eating, feet kicking, and sandal stomping, and just when the bibulous bunch thought they could drink no more, they did just that.

The women prepared the bridal tent. They covered the ground with carpets, perfumed the air with incense, and placed lamps, lit ever so dimly, on the table.

As the sun set, the stage was set for the magic moment. Rising branches became dancing silhouettes in the circle of the moonlight. Stars sat like diamonds on the velvet night sky. Laban fetched the heavily veiled bride and led her to the tent. She'd been kept out of sight all day. By the time it was time for Jacob to consummate his marriage, he was so drunk he could scarcely see what he was doing. At least that's the best way to explain how he fell for Laban's chicanery.

The next morning, with the fog cleared from his brain and the wine flushed out of his system, he rolled over in bed, expecting to see his lovely Rachel, and, holy cow, was he surprised! "Morning came: There was Leah in the marriage bed! Jacob confronted Laban: 'What have you done to me? Didn't I work all this time for the hand of Rachel? Why did you cheat me?'" (Gen. 29:25 THE MESSAGE).

Remember the phrase "a taste of your own medicine"? Jacob was handed a spoonful.

1. Jacob, who fooled his near-blind father, Isaac, in a tent, was fooled in a tent when he was blind on wine, blinded by night, blinded by lust, and blindly in love.
2. Jacob, who by the most calculating stealth stole what could not be returned, was tricked into a marriage that could not be undone.
3. Jacob, who begrudged and resisted the tradition of first-born going first, fell victim to Laban's explanation that it

was wrong "to give the younger before the firstborn" (Gen. 29:26).

4. Jacob, who complained to Laban, "Why did you cheat me?" (Gen. 29:25 THE MESSAGE), used the same word Esau used: "[Jacob] has cheated me these two times. He took away my birthright, and behold, now he has taken away my blessing" (Gen. 27:36 ESV).⁹

Confident that Jacob would agree, Laban offered to let Jacob marry Rachel as well. The condition? Seven more years of labor. Verse 28 is as terse as Jacob's expression must have been. "Jacob agreed" (THE MESSAGE). He finished the seven-day wedding with Leah and married Rachel. Something tells me the second party was a bit more subdued.

The chapter concludes with Jacob having sister wives—one wanted, the other not—seven more years of work to fulfill, and plenty of time to ponder a fundamental, recurring truth of Scripture: "You cannot cheat God. People harvest only what they plant" (Gal. 6:7 NCV).

Jacob planted seeds of deceit. He harvested the crop of deceit. He fooled Esau. He fooled Isaac. He was fooled by Laban. Jacob got "Jacobed."

I wish I could say he learned his lesson. What a delight it would be to write a paragraph like the following: "Jacob had an *aha* moment that rerouted his life for the better. He realized that he had spent his years dealing cards from the bottom of the deck and made a life change. Henceforth he treated every person with respect and honored God with reverence. Haran had its intended impact on Jacob."

But, alas, the paragraph would be fiction. Jacob remained stiff and unresponsive. Slow learner, this patriarch.

God sent him multiple messages. Some came in the form of blessings: A safe arrival in Haran. A stunning visage named Rachel. The ability to do the work of three men and move the rock from the well. Seven years of service that felt more like a delight than a duty. Could Jacob not have interpreted these gifts as indications that God was with him?

Other signals came in the form of burdens: His encounter with Laban the louse. The wedding night swap. Seven more years of hard work. At any point Jacob could have, should have, looked up. "Are you trying to tell me something, God?" God gave him plenty of opportunities to learn his lesson and change his ways. But he never did. Incredible.

And even more incredible, God never gave up on him. He never turned away. He never threw up his hands and quit.

Grace. Grace. Grace.

And you?

You find yourself far from home, far from hope, and far from the life you'd hoped to find. You're working hard on an advanced degree from the University of Hard Knocks, and graduation seems forever away. If that describes you, before you blame Laban or scowl at Leah, take a long look in the mirror. Let Jacob's story be a warning: we reap what we sow.

A parable of this principle is found in British landscape. The gardens of England are famed for their beauty. But only one holds the peculiar distinction of a garden designed to kill. Alnwick Garden in Northumberland boasts the typical scenery of primroses, lavish blooms, luscious ivy, and cascading fountains. Yet, if you journey deep into its heart, you'll find yourself beyond the black iron gates of the Poison Garden. Filled with approximately one hundred of the world's deadliest plants, this eerie plot requires strict rules for visitors, including no smelling, touching, or tasting. Every year incredulous tourists ignore the warning, and many faint from the deadly fragrances. What strikes most is the realization that so many of the deadly plants they encounter exist naturally alongside many they love. Both death and beauty sway in the wind as you walk through the park . . . and it all starts with just a little seed.[10]

What seeds are you sowing today? Just as seeds of deceit result in a harvest of deception, seeds of truth give way to a bountiful barnful of life. Consequences have compound interest.

You determine the quality of tomorrow by the seeds you sow today.

Jacob's story did not have to be routed through Haran. Marriage to the wrong sister was not mandated. Fourteen years of hard labor was not a requirement to be a patriarch. He could have completed God's plan and led a much more peaceful life.

But when we "sow the wind, [we] reap the whirlwind" (Hos. 8:7).

Or as the wise man stated: "When you're kind to others, you help yourself; when you're cruel to others, you hurt yourself. Bad work gets paid with a bad check; good work gets solid pay" (Prov. 11:17–18 THE MESSAGE).

Did Jacob learn his lesson? You'll need to keep reading about his life to find a definitive answer.

There is one redeeming detail in this honeymoon heist that needs to be mentioned. Remember Leah? The elder sister? The unwanted sister? The girl with the soft eyes and less fortunate name?

She gave birth to a son named Judah. Among her descendants were a shepherd boy of Bethlehem named David and a carpenter from Nazareth named Jesus. Yes, Leah, unchosen by Jacob, was chosen by God to be a mother in the bloodline of the King of kings.

Oh how the portraits of grace continue.

# CHAPTER 6

# DOMESTIC TURF WARS

---

Genesis 29:31–30:24

AT THE RIPE YOUNG AGE OF EIGHTY-TWO, MY oldest sister hosted a family reunion. Not wanting to leave anyone out, she issued an APB to Lucados worldwide. All were invited to spend a weekend hanging out under her roof in Fort Smith, Arkansas.

By the time Denalyn and I arrived, the place was abuzz with kith, kin, kids, and cousins. In-laws, outlaws, and a few fugitives of the law. There were some fifty or sixty of us, enough to require the wearing of name tags. I saw a few faces I'd never seen before and many I'd not seen in a long while. A couple were toothless and in diapers, but old age will do that to you.

My sister had accomplished the tedious task of designing a family tree and hanging it on her mantel. It stretched some six feet wide and covered a dozen decades and four generations. It began with the birth of my dad's dad and continued up to the most recent birth of my nephew's son.

She populated every possible corner of her living room with pictures of babies, brides, soldiers, farmers, and hairdressers—all bound by their connection to the Lucado clan.

My sisters and a cousin held high court, answering dozens of questions from the teens and newcomers.

"You mean he fought in World War II?"
"He went to prison?"
"Why didn't they have kids?"
"Why did they have so many kids?"

Our family tree has blight spots and bright spots. Alcohol and cholesterol have taken their toll. Education and better health habits have paid dividends.

In the final minutes before the final goodbyes, we crammed into the living room for one last look at the genealogy and one final question. "Has anyone learned anything this weekend?" After a few moments a great-grandson spoke up. Fresh out of college, having heard all the stories, he said, "I learned something. Now I know why I am the way I am."

We never escape our DNA. We may try, but we never succeed. While each life is a new chapter, it remains a chapter within a larger volume. Your biography began before you did. Your family matters.

Jacob's did. He was famous because of his family. He's not famous for his talents or treasures or teachings. If he invented a device, wrote a song, or authored a book, we've never seen, sung, or read it. But he seeded a family tree whose branches extend into eternity. Those who know little about the Bible have heard about the twelve tribes of Israel. Those who know a lot about the Bible are aware that the names of the tribes will be inscribed on the gates of the new Jerusalem (Rev. 21:12).

But even those who know a lot of the Bible have a lot of questions about the family of Jacob, the question at the top of the list being this one—*You mean to tell me that the genealogy of Jesus Christ includes these folks?*

We're already acquainted with the roller-coaster ride called Jacob's Life.

Jacob was the second born of Isaac, born second only a second after Esau. He came out of his mama trying to pull himself ahead of his brother. Sibling rivalry and parental favoritism resulted in a toxic stew of deception and death threats, and we aren't even into Jacob's marriages. Leah and Rachel, the two sister wives, each had a handmaiden who did more than their laundry. Jacob found himself in the midst of four women bearing his children and complicating his already turbulent and troubled life. His family gave scandal a bad name.

> When the LORD saw that Leah was not loved, he enabled her to conceive, but Rachel remained childless. Leah became pregnant and gave birth to a son. She named him Reuben, for she said, "It is because the LORD has seen my misery. Surely my husband will love me now."
>
> She conceived again, and when she gave birth to a son she said, "Because the LORD heard that I am not loved, he gave me this one too." So she named him Simeon.

Again she conceived, and when she gave birth to a son she said, "Now at last my husband will become attached to me, because I have borne him three sons." So he was named Levi.

She conceived again, and when she gave birth to a son she said, "This time I will praise the LORD." So she named him Judah. Then she stopped having children. (Gen. 29:31–35 NIV)

The naming of Leah's sons documented the hurt and hatred between the sister wives. Son number one's name, Reuben ("Look, a son"), was a sign that God had seen Leah's affliction. Simeon ("the LORD heard"), son number two's name, declared that God had heard Leah, a thinly veiled barb from Leah that God had not heard Rachel. The name Levi means "connect," lamenting Leah's lack of connection with Jacob, and Judah meant "Praise God."

The family was pregnant with tension about pregnancies and the lack thereof.

Leah had Jacob's sons but no love.

Rachel had Jacob's love but no sons.

Rachel, having witnessed her sister bear four sons, was so consumed with envy that she stormed into Jacob's tent, demanding, "Give me sons or I'll die" (Gen. 30:1 THE MESSAGE). Jacob mumbled something about the request not falling in his pay grade. Rachel took matters into her own hands and insisted, "Here's my maid Bilhah. Sleep with her. Let her substitute for me so I can have a child through her and build a family" (Gen. 30:3 THE MESSAGE).

Bilhah had a baby and named him—I assume with Rachel's input—Dan, which means "vindication." Or, in Texas slang, "Nanny nanny boo boo." Bilhah became pregnant a second time, and "Rachel said, 'I've been in an all-out fight with my sister—and I've won.' So she named him Naphtali (Fight)" (Gen. 30:7–8 THE MESSAGE).

Leah could no longer conceive, so she insisted that her maid Zilpah step in. "Zilpah had a son for Jacob. Leah said, 'How fortunate!' and she named him Gad (Lucky)." Then a second son. "Leah said, 'A happy day! The women will congratulate me in my happiness.' So she named him Asher (Happy)" (Gen. 30:10–13 THE MESSAGE).

Something tells me that Rachel did not congratulate Leah in her happiness.

The tone and turmoil of Jacob's dinner table must have been insane. Rachel and Leah despised each other. It was a battle of wills and wombs. The two handmaidens were rivals. Kids were born daily, it seemed. They were into everything: yammering, crying, crawling. No one could talk for the sound of them. Not that anyone wanted to talk. Everyone was at odds with everyone. Kindred, in their case, was dread of kin.

Just when we think the hornet's nest of domestic discord couldn't get more bizarre, it did exactly that. Reuben, the eldest son, found some mandrakes in the wheat field. In biblical times mandrakes were believed to be an aphrodisiac and to have fertility-producing powers.[1] Reuben gave them to his mother, Leah. Rachel heard about the mandrakes and asked Leah for them. "Leah said, 'Wasn't it enough that you got my husband away from me?'" (Gen. 30:15 THE MESSAGE).

By this point Jacob was full time with Rachel. Leah had been sleeping alone. So, in desperation, Rachel cut a deal with her sister. "If you will give me your son's mandrakes, you may sleep with Jacob tonight" (Gen. 30:15 NCV).

Somehow I missed this story in Sunday school. Take it to the core, and it's a case of Rachel pimping her husband to her sister. Go a level deeper, and it's a case of two women, each longing for something they'd yet to find. Both barren—one of affection, one of children.

And Jacob? Correct me if you disagree, but he seems so clueless. A little leadership wouldn't hurt. If only he'd taken a stand against Laban or taken up the cause of Leah or negotiated a truce between the sisters or when handed a handmaiden, said, "This crosses a line! Enough is enough!"

But the guy never did a thing. So indifferent. As glassy eyed as a speckled trout. Maybe he felt trapped in the middle of it all. An exile from his Beersheba home. An indentured servant to his uncle. Caught in the cross fire of two wives and two surrogates. Twelve children in seven years. Kids and chaos everywhere.

Sounds wild, right?

Sounds familiar, perhaps?

While writing this chapter, I received a call from a friend who asked, "What are you working on?" I answered, "I'm reading about Jacob's wacko family." Without skipping a beat, he offered, "Couldn't be more wacko than mine." I get it. The problem with using the phrase "dysfunctional family" is that it implies the existence of a functional one.

How many people find Jacob's story not only amazing but oddly assuring? In time Jacob would become the embodiment of the people of Israel. He did so, not because of his nature, but in spite of it. Scripture makes no attempt to whitewash his scandal, to gloss over the flaws, or to hide the humanness. I, for one, find hope in the ability of God to use a family of feuds and friction.

I'm reminded of a framed X-ray I keep in my closet. As I sort through my socks and select my shirt, it greets me. Odd, I know. Other people hang calendars and favorite quotes. But I have a framed X-ray. Here's why.

The picture is an axial view of a decimated hip. A jarring car crash left it broken in two places. Even an untrained eye like mine can spot the quarter-inch gap between the bones. The breakage was just one of several the victim suffered. Doctors who studied the X-ray feared for her life. Even more so, they feared for the life of her child. An unborn, seven-month-old infant occupies center stage of the X-ray. He floats amidst the fracture, blissfully unaware of the breakage around him.

Dr. Michael Wirth, who gave me the image, remembers the night he saw it in the emergency room. "We wondered, 'Can both mother and child survive? If not, do we take the mother and lose the child? Lose the mother and save the child?'"

They never had to make the choice. The mother lived, the baby was delivered, and Michael kept the X-ray as a reminder: God delivers life through brokenness. Broken families, hearts, dreams—even broken people. We crack under pressure. Like Esau, we cave in to the cravings that gnaw at our guts. Like Jacob, we connive and control. Who wants to use a broken vessel? God does. His grace never quits.

A person might read about Jacob's clan and ask, "Where are the heroes? Who am I supposed to be emulating? Who is the redeeming character in this polygamous mess?" The answer: God! Where you and I see a family that spends more time at each other's throats than in each other's arms, God sees an opportunity to display his strength—"Watch what I can do."

God used, and uses, flawed people. He made a promise to Abraham: his children would be like dust on the earth and stars in the galaxies. The greatest person who ever lived would spring from his loins. The story of heaven would be told and distributed through these odd and curious people. God had made them a promise. He never breaks his promises.

Case in point: the family of Jacob.

Dysfunctional families can be used, even fixed. Function can happen. Good intentions to love can become real. God can flick everything into healing mode. No family is beyond the possibility of a miracle.

Rachel eventually got pregnant. Was it the mandrakes? No, it was God. "God remembered Rachel. God listened to her and opened her womb. She became pregnant and had a son. She said, 'God has taken away my humiliation.' She named him Joseph" (Gen. 30:22–24 THE MESSAGE).

Through the squabbling, strutting, struggling, competing, and comparing; the love potions, surrogate strategies, and tears of the loveless and the childless, God was in control. He delivered on his word then.

He delivers on his word still.

CHAPTER 7

# LIFE WITH A LOUSE

---

Genesis 30:25–31:55

## LET'S TALK ABOUT THE LABAN IN YOUR LIFE.

I know. You'd rather not. You'd rather talk about something—someone—more pleasant. Your Laban is anything but pleasant.

Your Laban is demanding. He has the sensitivity of a rabid pit bull.

Your Laban is conniving. She breaks promises like a short-order cook cracks eggs.

Your Laban is deceptive. There's always a card up his sleeve or fingers crossed behind her back.

Your Laban is manipulative. He'll flatter you until he gets what he wants then move on to someone else.

Your Laban loves to be adored. "Enough of me talking about me. What about you? You talk about me."

Your Laban is streptococcus on the tonsils of your life. You'd like a day without him, but you're stuck. Your Laban is your in-law. Your Laban is your boss. Your Laban sits in the next cubicle or plays on the same team.

A future with no Laban, for the time, is not an option. Maybe you wonder why in the world God has a Laban in yours.

Jacob asked himself the question at least once a day for 5,110 days—the number of days he'd worked for the man. Fourteen years! He could not escape him. He'd married Laban's daughters, for goodness sake.

The original agreement was for seven years, but Laban pulled a wedding night shell trick, swapping Rachel with her older sister, Leah, and leaving Jacob with no option but to work seven more years.

In the Bible the number seven often signifies "complete." Appropriate symbolism because Jacob surely felt like a complete fool working for less than minimum wage for a man who traded his daughters like a cattleman trades livestock at the stock show.

During the second set of seven years, Jacob saw his family and his troubles multiply. He gained eleven sons and one daughter: seven children by Leah, one by Rachel, two by Rachel's maid, Bilhah, and two by Leah's maid, Zilpah. Jacob had arrived in Laban's camp with nothing, and after fourteen stress-filled years, his headaches had increased, but his bank account had not.

Ten times in six years Laban altered his method of computing Jacob's wages, leaving Jacob empty-handed (Gen. 31:41–42). Is this how God rewards his children? Is this how God keeps his promises? What happened to the ladder that led into heaven?

Where are the ascending and descending angels? Why can't one of them pluck Laban and plop him into someone else's life?

Where is God in the midst of this chaos?

The answer came in the form of a dream—an odd one, but dreams often are. Jacob told Leah and Rachel about it.

> In breeding season I once had a dream in which I looked up and saw that the male goats mating with the flock were streaked, speckled or spotted. The angel of God said to me in the dream, "Jacob." I answered, "Here I am." And he said, "Look up and see that all the male goats mating with the flock are streaked, speckled or spotted, for I have seen all that Laban has been doing to you. I am the God of Bethel, where you anointed a pillar and where you made a vow to me. Now leave this land at once and go back to your native land." (Gen. 31:10–13 NIV)

Set aside the curious comments about streaked, speckled, and spotted sheep. They matter, and we will return to them in a few paragraphs. But they matter less than the big news that God shared with Jacob: "I have seen all that Laban has been doing to you."

*I have not turned away. I have not forgotten your plight. I have not dismissed your need. I . . . have . . . seen!*

Jacob was left with two options: trust God or grow anxious. He could either believe in the presence of heaven or heed the presence of problems. If you assume he focused on his problems, no one would fault you. Jacob has done little thus far to show his faith.

Yet we are about to see a change in the man. A change for the better (albeit momentary). We've waited a decade and a half to say those words! We've seen the swindler swindle his brother and cheat his father. We've seen the fugitive stumble into Laban's camp. We've seen the lover so drunk on love and liquor he wakes up with the wrong bride in a story as scrambled as a spilled Scrabble box. We've seen the passive husband sit in silence as his wives squabble and their hearts break. We've seen him reap what he sowed. But finally something within Jacob begins to stir. He turns in his resignation to his father-in-law.

> After Rachel had had Joseph, Jacob spoke to Laban, "Let me go back home. Give me my wives and children for whom I've served you. You know how hard I've worked for you."
>
> Laban said, "If you please, I have learned through divine inquiry that GOD has blessed me because of you." He went on, "So name your wages. I'll pay you." (Gen. 30:25–28 THE MESSAGE)

Laban was not a man of faith. He was not a seeker of God. Yet Laban was getting richer each year. He couldn't figure out why. He sought an explanation through "divine inquiry." He checked his tarot cards and consulted palm readers. He rolled dice and read tea leaves. Finally he realized the house of Laban prospered because of the presence of Jacob. "GOD has blessed me because of you" (Gen. 30:27 THE MESSAGE).

Life with a Laban can leave us wondering if we are making a difference. The truth is, we aren't, but God is! Wherever we go, we carry God's blessings with us, blessings that overflow into the lives of others.[1] How good of God! He wants to bless even the Labans of the world. He uses the Jacobs to do so.

Jacob told his father-in-law, "You know well what my work has meant to you and how your livestock has flourished under my care. The little you had when I arrived has increased greatly; everything I did resulted in blessings for you. Isn't it about time that I do something for my own family?" (vv. 29–30 THE MESSAGE).

In other words, "Laban, I took your business from a corner store to a multimillion-dollar operation. Whatever I touched, the Lord blessed. Under my direction your income has multiplied. But now it is time for me to care for my family."

Laban, tight as the strings of a tennis racket, asked, "So, what should I pay you?"

Jacob said, "You don't have to pay me a thing. But how about this? I will go back to pasture and care for your flocks. Go through your entire flock today and take out every speckled or spotted sheep, every dark-colored lamb, every spotted or speckled goat. They will be my wages. That way you can check on my honesty when you assess my wages. If you find any goat that's not speckled or spotted or a sheep that's not black, you will know that I stole it." (Gen. 30:31–33 THE MESSAGE)

Remember the dream? In it God told Jacob to build a flock with streaked, speckled, or spotted animals. So Jacob obeyed. He offered to take as his wages a handful of dotted sheep and goats. Laban couldn't believe his ears. No wonder Jacob was broke. A shepherd can't get rich by taking just a few marked sheep and goats.

Laban thought Jacob was a fool. Jacob, however, was acting in faith.

"Fair enough," said Laban. "It's a deal." But that very day Laban removed all the mottled and spotted billy goats and all the speckled and spotted nanny goats, every animal that had even a touch of white on it plus all the black sheep and placed them under the care of his sons. Then he put a three-day journey between himself and Jacob. Meanwhile Jacob went on tending what was left of Laban's flock. (Gen. 30:34–36 THE MESSAGE)

Before Jacob had a chance to cull the flocks, Laban purged them of the speckled and spotted sheep. Together with his sons and workers, he scampered up and down the hills snatching the dark and spotted ones. Laban then sent the sheep off on a three-day journey to a distant pasture. Jacob was left with a fraction of his promised wages. Ever the shark, Laban cheated Jacob again.

Can't we envision Laban, smug and pigeon chested with pride, talking to himself as he swayed side to side on his camel. "Maybe your God forgot you this time, Jacob?"

Can't we envision Jacob coming ever so close to lashing out against Laban? It wasn't enough for the man to cheat him at the wedding. It wasn't enough for Laban to force Jacob to work for nothing. It wasn't enough for Laban to take advantage of his own son-in-law. Laban had to leave Jacob with next to nothing!

But Jacob didn't react in anger. Instead, he set about the task of building his flock. He took "fresh branches from poplar, almond, and plane trees and peeled the bark, leaving white stripes on them. He stuck the peeled branches in front of the watering troughs where the flocks came to drink. When the flocks were in heat, they came to drink and mated in front of the streaked branches. Then they gave birth to young that were streaked or spotted or speckled" (Gen. 30:37–39 THE MESSAGE).

What is going on here? Was this superstition? Folklore? Or

was Jacob ahead of his time? Some scholars think so. "It has been recently proposed that . . . Jacob's stripping the bark from the branches may have exposed some nutrient that was then in the drinking water . . . thereby changing the colour of the coats of the young that they bore."[2]

Over the next six years Jacob put this unique breeding plan to work. "[Jacob] got richer and richer, acquiring huge flocks, lots and lots of servants, not to mention camels and donkeys" (Gen. 30:43 THE MESSAGE).

God rewarded Jacob's faith! God used Laban to teach Jacob to trust God. Jacob didn't like Laban. He wanted to leave Laban. Yet he was better because of Laban.

Laban was Jacob's catfish. Research the phrase "catfish and codfish," and you'll find this apocryphal, yet insightful, tale.

Fishermen struggled to find a way to deliver codfish to market. They tried freezing them, but the fish lost its flavor. They tried transporting them in a seawater tank. The codfish would be inactive too long, making it soft and mushy. Finally someone came up with a solution. Catfish and codfish are natural enemies. A catfish was placed in the tank. It chased the codfish during the transport, resulting in the delivery of healthy cod.

Great story. While there's no proof that fishermen use catfish, there's ample evidence that God does.

In Jacob's story Laban was Jacob's catfish.

And you? Might God be saying the same words to you he said to Jacob? "I see what is happening. I know about the manipulation. The unfairness. The disregard for your feelings or future. I see it. I see you. And I am using this experience to train you."

God is prone to do this. Scripture explains, "This trouble

you're in isn't punishment; it's *training*, the normal experience of children. . . . God is doing what *is* best for us, training us to live God's holy best" (Heb. 12:8, 10 THE MESSAGE, emphasis in the original).

Are you being trained?

You, like Jacob, are part of God's delivery system of hope. You are a courier of his covenant. Yet, you, like Jacob, have your share of foibles and flaws.

So "God is *at work in you*, both to will and to work for his good pleasure" (Phil. 2:13 RSV, emphasis mine). He will "equip you with everything good that you may do his will, *working in you* that which is pleasing in his sight" (Heb. 13:21 RSV, emphasis mine).

We are the rough stones; he is the lapidary. We are the bent timber. He is the carpenter.

Rather than grumble about the people who irritate you, see them for what they are—God's training tool. He is teaching you to trust him. He hasn't promised to give you striped sheep. But he has promised to . . .

- anoint you with the oil of gladness. (Ps. 45:7)
- supply all your needs according to his riches in glory by Christ Jesus. (Phil. 4:19)
- bless you with good measure, pressed down, shaken together, running over. (Luke 6:38)
- grant sufficient grace. (2 Cor. 12:9)
- make all things work together for good. (Rom. 8:28)
- defeat any weapon that is forged against you. (Isa. 54:17)
- provide streams in the desert. (Isa. 43:19)
- make a way when there is no way. (Isa. 43:16)

- turn sorrow into joy. (Ps. 30:11)
- bind up your broken heart. (Ps. 147:3)

At some point someone somewhere is going to boil your blood. He or she may not be a true scoundrel like Laban, but even those closest to you will let an insult fly now and again. The temptation is to retaliate, to use your head in a less-than-rational way. Don't give in. Don't fight Laban on Laban's terms. Respond to Laban with faith in God.

Jacob did. At the end of six years, Jacob had enough riches and had had enough of Laban. So he loaded up and left for Canaan.

Laban pursued him. He accused Jacob of being a thief. Two decades of frustration fired out of Jacob like a howitzer spits bullets.

I have been with you for twenty years now. Your sheep and goats have not miscarried, nor have I eaten rams from your flocks. I did not bring you animals torn by wild beasts; I bore the loss myself. And you demanded payment from me for whatever was stolen by day or night. This was my situation: The heat consumed me in the daytime and the cold at night, and sleep fled from my eyes. It was like this for the twenty years I was in your household. I worked for you fourteen years for your two daughters and six years for your flocks, and you changed my wages ten times. If the God of my father, the God of Abraham and the Fear of Isaac, had not been with me, you would surely have sent me away empty-handed. But God has seen my hardship and the toil of my hands, and last night he rebuked you. (Gen. 31:38–42 NIV)

Jacob had fulfilled his fourteen years. He absorbed the losses. Endured the bad weather and weathered the bad times. Laban did not disagree. He could not disagree. Jacob not only survived his season with Laban; he thrived. He had developed a deeper faith. He declared for all to hear, "God has seen my hardship." God used Laban to shape Jacob.

Is God using your Laban to shape you?

You'd prefer a life with no Laban. Who wouldn't?

But life comes with Labans. If this season has one chasing you around the tank, remember: God uses peculiar people to bring out the best in his people.

Try this: *Talk to God about your Laban.* Ask him, "Lord, what lessons are you teaching me through this catfish?"

And this: *Thank God for your Laban.* "When troubles of any kind come your way, consider it an opportunity for great joy. For you know that when your faith is tested, your endurance has a chance to grow" (James 1:2–3 NLT).

Life's Labans can make you want to pull your hair out— but they can also make you desperate for God. And that's an invaluable blessing. So the next time life gives you Labans . . . you know what to do!

Your Laban will not be around forever. The day is soon coming when you, like Jacob, will be released. Till then, trust God's purpose and promise.

You'll be better because of it.

CHAPTER 8

# FACE-TO-FACE WITH YOURSELF

Genesis 32:1–32

- You thought you had the wherewithal to save your career. Just log more hours, call on more clients, put in more effort. For years the approach worked. But then the walls collapsed. The economy nose-dived. The company went under, and it threatens to take you with it. All of a sudden you feel your world spinning out of control.
- Your marriage has always been a challenge, yet the two of you have kept it together. Little by little, however, the bridge has eroded. You're running out of cope, running low on hope. For the last few weeks you've hardly spoken. You share the same house but not the same heart. It's a wrestling match, this marriage.

- You've kept your addiction a secret. You've mastered the ability to appear sober. You know which vodka to drink and which mouthwash to use. You convinced yourself you could manage. But you didn't see the stoplight. Now the car is a wreck, and so are you. You've never known the inside of a jail cell before. You will tonight.

**LIFE COMES WITH INFLECTION POINTS, JUNCTURES** in which we know our world is about to change. Events that time-stamp life. Crossroads that demand a decision. Go this way? Or that? Everyone has them. You do. I do. Jacob did. Jacob's came with a name: Jabbok.

By this point Jacob had bidden adieu to Laban. Mesopotamia was in his rearview mirror. He'd arrived a man on the lam, only his staff in hand, fleeing his behemoth brother. He left two decades later with four women, eleven sons, and one daughter. He led a tribe of servants and droves of sheep, cattle, goats, and camels.

We are not told if Jacob thought of Esau during his exile. But he must have. Jacob must have feared the rage that awaited him upon his return. He'd hoodwinked the birthright from his older brother and turned Esau into the laughingstock of the clan. The last time Jacob heard Esau's name, it was couched in panic. His mother had warned, "Get out before your brother kills you!"

Esau would have.

By now the older brother was a squire of sorts. His household numbered in the hundreds and flocks in the thousands. Jacob could not survive in Canaan apart from Esau's favor. Would Esau be resolute on revenge? Or would he let bygones be bygones?

That was the concern on Jacob's mind as he headed south

through the hills on the eastern side of the Jordan River near Jabbok.

So God gave Jacob some assurance. He revealed the army of angels that surrounded him. "And Jacob went his way. Angels of God met him. When Jacob saw them he said, 'Oh! God's Camp!' And he named the place Mahanaim (Campground)" (Gen. 32:1–2 THE MESSAGE).

The word used here for *camp* appears elsewhere in Scripture to describe hundreds of thousands of soldiers (1 Chron. 12:22). When Jacob left Canaan, the angels met him (Gen. 28:12), and then upon his return, they met him again. Rank upon rank, they moved in the sky like iridescent waves of the aurora borealis. Perhaps it was their presence that gave Jacob the courage to send servants ahead to his brother.

> He told them, "Give this message to my master Esau: 'Humble greetings from your servant Jacob. . . . I have sent these messengers to inform my lord of my coming, hoping that you will be friendly to me.'" (Gen. 32:4–5 NLT).

Do you hear the language of Jacob? "My master Esau . . . ," "inform my lord . . . ," "hoping that you will be friendly to me . . ." Jacob, at least in dialect, came in humility, pleading for mercy. Did his appeal make a difference? Read the next verse and see what you think.

> The messengers came back to Jacob and said, "We talked to your brother Esau and he's on his way to meet you. But he has four hundred men with him." (Gen. 32:6 THE MESSAGE)

*Gulp.* Four hundred clansmen thundered toward Jacob. But that's no problem. An army of angels hovered above him. Jacob gathered himself, told his family not to fear, and moved forward, right? Not quite.

> Jacob was scared. Very scared. Panicked, he divided his people, sheep, cattle, and camels into two camps. He thought, "If Esau comes on the first camp and attacks it, the other camp has a chance to get away." (Gen. 32:7–8 THE MESSAGE)

Oh, how Jacob could vacillate. Communing with angels in one instance, frightened by soldiers the next. Our hero had more waffles in him than IHOP.

Yet, lest we be too hard on Jacob, hurry to the next passage. Jacob, for the first time that we know of in twenty years, offered a prayer. And a wonderful prayer it is!

> O God of my father Abraham and God of my father Isaac, O LORD who said to me, "Return to your country and to your kindred, that I may do you good," I am not worthy of the least of all the deeds of steadfast love and all the faithfulness that you have shown to your servant, for with only my staff I crossed this Jordan, and now I have become two camps. Please deliver me from the hand of my brother, from the hand of Esau, for I fear him, that he may come and attack me, the mothers with the children." (Gen. 32:9–11 ESV)

Who is this Jacob? He prays like a man who depends on God's goodness. Has he learned the Laban lesson? He reminded God of the promises God had made. He acknowledged that he was unworthy of God's unfailing grace and faithfulness. He gave God credit for his abundant wealth. And then he said, in so many words, *If you don't help me, I'm burnt toast.*

Jacob kicked into high gear, desperate to avert a bloodbath. He began sending gifts to Esau. One drove after another of flocks: goats, ewes, lambs, camels, bulls, donkeys. He sent some 550 animals arranged in six groups.

Jacob instructed the herdsmen to tell Esau that "your servant Jacob is on his way behind us" (Gen. 32:20 THE MESSAGE). The Hebrew word used here for "servant" was to acknowledge a status of inferiority;[1] as if Jacob were saying, "I'm a jerk. I'm a chump. You're the class act in the family." Within short order the gifts were delivered. He sent everyone across the river and stayed behind to spend the night alone.

In my opinion what happened next warrants a place in the great hall of holy moments: Moses on Mount Sinai. Elijah on Mount Carmel. Jesus in the Jordan River and on Mount Calvary. You make your list. I'll make mine, but let's make sure both lists include Jacob at Jabbok.

*Jabbok.* The very name of the river has a thrust to it. *Jab! Buck!* Jacob is about to be jabbed and bucked for the entire night.

> But Jacob stayed behind by himself, and a man wrestled with him until daybreak. When the man saw that he couldn't get the best of Jacob as they wrestled, he deliberately threw Jacob's hip out of joint.
>
> The man said, "Let me go; it's daybreak."
>
> Jacob said, "I'm not letting you go 'til you bless me."

The man said, "What's your name?"

He answered, "Jacob."

The man said, "But no longer. Your name is no longer Jacob. From now on it's Israel (God-Wrestler); you've wrestled with God and you've come through." (Gen. 32:24–28 THE MESSAGE)

This passage is as mysterious as the stranger it describes. Here is where my imagination takes me.

Someone grabbed Jacob around the neck and threw him to the ground. Jacob jumped up and jumped at him, driving his shoulder into the gut of the attacker until the two fell flat. The stranger pushed him off and pounced on Jacob, pressing his shoulders into the muddy bank.

Back and forth the two struggled. Jabbok's water surging. The night wind howling. The duo grunting, elbowing, scraping, clawing, straddling, and wrestling. Jowl to jowl.

Jacob on top.

The stranger on top.

Jacob tried to run. The attacker dragged him back. Bodies slippery with mud. Skin wet with sweat. They said no words. They panted like stallions. They leapt like gazelles. A blur of fury. Flipping, slipping, dodging, and wrestling.

Jacob had always handled his problems on his own. Did he not survive the walk through the wilderness? Outlast Laban and his tricks? Amass a fortune and a clan? He fought his own fights. He was savvy, smart, and slippery. He'd made a life of coming out on top. He'd do it again.

But the Man would not retreat.

Hours passed. On and on through the night they wrestled.

Finally Jacob saw the first shudder of a sunrise on a distant hill. "When the man saw that he would not win the match, he touched Jacob's hip and wrenched it out of its socket" (v. 25 NLT).

Who was this stranger? Jacob would later say, "I have seen God face to face, yet my life has been spared" (Gen. 32:30 NLT).

Did Jacob actually prevail against God? The answer is yes, until God made his point.

God let Jacob fight until it appeared that Jacob was in control. Then, with one touch, God dislocated the hip, leaving Jacob to limp back to his family. It's as if God said, "That's enough, Jacob." He touched Jacob with a force that Jacob had never felt. Jacob crumpled to the ground, broken and humbled.

I see symbolism in this injury. The hip is the largest weight-bearing joint in the body, and it engages some of the strongest muscles. Yet it was putty at the touch of the Stranger. What's more, this damage to Jacob's hip was more than damage to a joint. The word used in this text can refer to vital organs.[2] The touch left Jacob's manhood redefined.

The message of the dislocation? "You aren't as strong as you think. Rely on me."

Do you know the mud of Jabbok?

I do. My journal entries don't use the river's name. But they certainly speak of occasions in which I've wrestled with God.

One of the most dramatic occurred some twenty years ago; I was about fifty years old. To the casual observer I was on top of the world. Our brand-new church sanctuary was bursting at the seams. We added new members every week. The congregation had very little debt and absolutely no doubt that their pastor was doing a great work.

Our church actually appeared on the list of popular San Antonio attractions. Tour companies bused tourists to our services. The magazine *Christianity Today* sent a reporter to write a profile on me. The writer called me "America's Pastor." *Reader's Digest* designated me as the "Best Preacher in America."

All cylinders were firing. I turned sermons into books. My publisher turned books into arena events. I wrote kids stories and recorded kids videos. It was wild!

What no one knew was this: I was a mess.

Our staff was struggling. Departments were squaring off against one another. Tacky emails were flying like missiles. Ministers were competing for budget dollars. A couple of invaluable employees, weary from the tension, quietly resigned. And since I was the senior pastor, it fell to me to set things in order.

Yet, who had time for intramural squabbles? I had lessons to prepare. The problem with Sundays is that they happen each week! In addition I led a midweek prayer service and taught a weekly early morning men's gathering. Deadlines were coming at me from all sides. I needed time to think, to pray, to study.

What's more (or consequently) I was unhealthy. My heart had the rhythm of a Morse code message: irregular and inconsistent. The cardiologist diagnosed me with atrial fibrillation, put me on medicine, and told me to slow down. But how could I?

The staff needed me.

The pulpit required me.

The publisher was counting on me.

The entire world was looking to me.

So I did what came naturally. I began to drink.

Not publicly. I was the guy you see at the convenience store who buys the big can of beer, hides it in a sack, and presses it against his thigh so no one will see as he hurries out the door. My store of choice was on the other side of the city lest I be seen. I'd sit in the car, pull the can out of the sack, and guzzle the liquid until it took the edge off the sharp demands of the day.

That's how "America's Pastor" was coping with his world gone crazy.

My Jabbok, as it turned out, was a parking lot. The wrestling match lasted for the better part of an hour on a spring afternoon. I told God I had everything under control. The staff issues were manageable. The deadlines were manageable. The stress was manageable. The drinking was manageable. But then came a moment of truth. God didn't touch my hip, but he spoke to my heart. *Really, Max? If you have everything together, if you have a lock on this issue, then why are you hiding in a parking lot, sipping a beer that you've concealed in a brown paper bag?*

Jabbok. That moment in which God brings you face-to-face with yourself, and what you see you don't like.

Jabbok. When you use all your strength, only to find your strength won't give you what you need.

Jabbok. A single touch on the hip that brings you to your knees.

Jabbok. Jab. Buck.

Yet even in the moment, or especially in that moment, God dispensed grace. Look what happened next to Jacob.

"What is your name?" the man asked. He replied, "Jacob." (Gen. 32:27 NLT)

On the page of your Bible, there is scarcely a space between the question and the reply. In real time, however, I sense a pause, a long, painful pause. *What is your name?* There was only one answer, and Jacob choked to spit it out. *My . . . name . . . is . . . Jacob.* This was a confession. Jacob was admitting to God that he was, indeed, a *Jacob*: a heel, a cheater, a hustler, a smart operator, a fraud. "That's who I am. I'm a Jacob."

> "Your name will no longer be Jacob," the man told him. "From now on you will be called Israel, because you have fought with God and with men and have won." (v. 28 NLT)

Of all the times to be given a new name. And of all the times to be given *this* name.[3] *Israel* means "God fights" or "God strives." The name celebrated, and celebrates, God's power and loyalty.

The old Jacob fought for himself. The old Jacob relied on his wits, trickery, and fast feet. Jacob, himself, took care of himself. The new Jacob had a new source of power: God. From this day forward each introduction would be a reminder of God's presence. "Hello, my name is God fights." Each call to dinner a welcome instruction, "God fights, it's time to eat." His email address was godfights@israel.com. His business card reminded all who read it of the true power of Israel: "God fights." His old name reflected his old self. His new name reflected his new strength. "God fights."

What grace.

God extended it to me. Abundantly. I confessed my hypocrisy to our elders, and they did what good pastors do. They covered me with prayer and designed a plan to help me cope with demands.

I admitted my struggle to the congregation and in doing so activated a dozen or so conversations with members who battled the same temptation.

We no longer see tour buses in our parking lot, and that's fine with me. I enjoy an occasional beer—but for flavor, not stress management. And if anyone mentions the "America's Pastor" moniker, an image comes to mind. The image of a weary, lonely preacher in a convenience store parking lot.

God met me there that day. He gave me a new name as well. Not Israel. That one was already taken. But "forgiven." And I'm happy to wear it.

# CHAPTER 9

# PAST TENSE

Genesis 33

**FRED SNODGRASS LED AN EXTRAORDINARY LIFE.** During his more than eight decades, he played nine years of professional baseball. He succeeded as a rancher and a banker. He served as mayor of Oxnard, California. He was an exemplary family man and a model citizen.

Yet when he passed away in 1974, the obituary headline did not highlight his achievements. The *New York Times* heralded his most famous failure: "Fred Snodgrass, 86, Dead Ball Player Muffed 1912 Fly."[1]

It's true. Snodgrass dropped the fly ball in the last game of the 1912 World Series. Had he caught the tenth-inning pop-up, the New York Giants would have won the title. But Snodgrass took his eye off the ball. It fell to the ground. His error led to two runs, a lost game, and a mistake that would follow him to the grave.

We've done the same. Not in the outfield of a baseball game but in . . . Would you care to fill in the blank?

- a marriage
- a business
- your youth
- your parenting

We didn't let the ball fall, but we let our spouse down, our guard down, our debt spiral out of control. We live, not with the stigma of a lost game, but with a divided family, a broken heart, or an angry brother.

That was the case with Jacob.

He and Esau were twins, you'll recall, separated in age by the length of time it took for Jacob to exit the womb. Jacob resented the second-place finish, and when he saw an opportunity to reverse the situation, he took it. He caught Esau with a hungry belly and in a flippant mood and convinced him to swap his birthright for a bowl of stew. Jacob achieved what he wanted but burned bridges to get it.

When we last left Esau, the storm raged in him like lava in Krakatoa. He muttered about Jacob.

"Not for nothing was he named Jacob, the Heel. Twice now he's tricked me: first he took my birthright and now he's taken my blessing. . . ." Esau seethed in anger against Jacob because of the blessing his father had given him; he brooded, "The time for mourning my father's death is close. And then I'll kill my brother Jacob." (Gen. 27:36, 41 THE MESSAGE)

Jacob got wind of Esau's anger and hightailed it to the high country to hide out while Esau cooled down. Now it was time to face him.

God told him, "Return to the land of your father and grandfather and to your relatives there, and I will be with you" (Gen. 31:3 NLT). In order to return to the land, Jacob had to return to the region where Esau lived. No more hiding. No more running. Jacob might have been happy to sidestep the encounter, but not God. Meeting Esau was a spiritual necessity.

To move forward into his future, Jacob had to come face-to-face with his past.

He's not the only Bible hero to have a sordid story in his or her biography. Moses had blood on his hands from murdering an Egyptian (Ex. 2:12). Abraham lied about his wife, passing her off as a sister in order to save his neck (Gen. 12:12–13). Elijah, the prophet, had enough faith to call down fire one day and enough fear to drive him into hiding the next (1 Kings 18–19). Esther took a courageous stand but not before she didn't. She hid her Jewish identity from the king (Est. 2:20).

Got some stains on your past? Peter can relate. On the night Christ needed him most, the disciple cursed the very name of Jesus (Matt. 26:69–75). Paul had skeletons in his closet. The apostle whose words we cherish, study, and memorize? He himself confessed, "I persecuted the people who followed the Way of Jesus, and some of them were even killed. I arrested men and women and put them in jail" (Acts 22:4 NCV). Paul actively tried to "destroy the church" (Acts 8:3 NIV). The Greek word for "destroy" denotes a brutal and sadistic cruelty.[2] His aggression was no mere lapse in judgment or youthful indiscretion.

Moses had blood on his hands.

Abraham was a bald-faced liar.

Elijah was a coward.

Jacob was a liar and a cheat.

Esther kept her faith a secret.

Peter was a betrayer.

Paul was a murderer.

Yet God used them all. They chose to trust God with their futures and because they did, their pasts no longer had a hold on them.

God's not put off by our ugly chapter(s). With his help we can soon say what Paul came to say: "But one thing I do: forgetting what lies behind and straining forward to what lies ahead, I press on toward the goal for the prize of the upward call of God in Christ Jesus" (Phil. 3:13–14 ESV).

Paul put his past in the past and set his eyes on the future. Want to do likewise? Take some notes on Jacob's story.

On the big day of the Esau encounter, the exhausted, God-struck patriarch limped back to his camp. "Esau was coming, and with him were four hundred men" (Gen. 33:1). He could see Esau in the distance, across the field. The big, brawny brother walked a dozen steps ahead of his militia. His beard still red. His arms still thick. A bow and a quiver slung across his back. It was Jacob, the dachshund, vs. Esau, the Doberman.

The next few actions leave us wondering if the old Jacob or the new Israel was in charge.

He sent his family out first. He divided his children among their mothers. He placed them in a sequence: first, Bilhah and

Zilpah, the handmaidens. Next Leah, the wife he didn't want. Finally, Rachel, the wife he loved, and their son, Joseph. The meaning was lost on no one. That was a Jacob decision.

But then, signs of the new Israel. "He crossed over before them and bowed himself to the ground seven times, until he came near to his brother" (Gen. 33:3).

Jacob, in his folly, might have run to hide.

Israel, with the limp, had no choice but to trust. He prostrated himself like a vassal before a royal in an ancient court. A few steps then nose and forehead on the ground. A few more steps then face on the ground. Five more times he lowered himself to the earth. Obsequious to the extreme. And then all of a sudden "Esau ran to meet him, and embraced him, and fell on his neck and kissed him, and they wept" (Gen. 33:4).

When Esau rejected his birthright, the narrator described the moment with five percussive verbs: *"ate . . . drank . . . got up . . . left . . . despised"* (25:34 NIV). Now, in the moment of reconciliation, he rapidly fires five verbs of opposite sentiment: *"ran . . . embraced . . . fell . . . kissed . . . wept."*

Esau squeezed him so close Israel nearly lost his breath. Esau released him long enough to look at his face. The eyes of the twins met for the first time in twenty years.

Both sets filled with tears, and they wept.

They wept for relief.

They wept with forgiveness.

They wept at the possibility of a new start, a fresh beginning.

Esau wept because his brother was home.

Israel wept because he'd come face-to-face with his past only to find that his past held no power over his life.

God had gone ahead of him. God had kept the promise he had made in Bethel: "I am with you and will keep you wherever you go, and will bring you back to this land" (Gen. 28:15).

The journey came at God's behest and with God's provision. He sent angels to welcome Jacob into the land. He blessed Jacob with a new name. He stripped Jacob of human power, leaving him to rely on God. God softened the heart of Esau. This is not a story of Jacob's courage. It is a story of "the Almighty's single-minded dedication to love humanity and to implement his plan through flawed persons."[3]

God led Jacob into his future by helping him face his past.

Don't we need him to do the same for us?

We can relate to the words of Paul. "No matter which way I turn I can't make myself do right. I want to but I can't. When I want to do good, I don't; and when I try not to do wrong, I do it anyway. . . . Oh, what a terrible predicament I'm in! Who will free me from my slavery to this deadly lower nature?" (Rom. 7:18–19, 24 TLB).

Paul's past was quicksand. The more he struggled, the deeper he sank. Just when we think he is about to go under, he announced: "Thanks be to God, who delivers me through Jesus Christ our Lord! . . . Therefore, there is now no condemnation for those who are in Christ Jesus" (7:25; 8:1 NIV).

Paul discovered a guilt-free zone. Through Jesus, every chain and shackle fell to the ground. Paul moved past his past. No small matter for a murderer, church divider, and self-proclaimed hypocrite. Yet he trusted God with his future and moved on.

Do likewise.

"If we confess our sins, he will forgive our sins, because we can trust God to do what is right. He will cleanse us from all the wrongs we have done" (1 John 1:9 NCV). Note who is active in this passage: "he will forgive our sins . . . we can trust God to do what is right . . . he will cleanse us." The remedy for our sin is not our work but God's work. Tell Christ what you did. Be specific. Hold nothing back. No sin is too ancient, evil, or insignificant. You were not made to carry this weight. Only Jesus can take it away. Ask him to do so. Take your guilt in your hand as if it were a stone, and hand it to him.

"Jesus, will you please take this from me?"

You know how he will respond. "Come to Me, all who are weary and burdened, and I will give you rest" (Matt. 11:28 NASB).

Paul Hegstrom accepted this invitation. His past was a shameful one. Within a week of his wedding, he began beating his wife. Bouts of rage led to violence on an almost weekly basis. When children came, he beat them. After sixteen years of marriage, his wife gave up and got out.

The divorce was not enough of a wake-up call. His unmanaged anger ruined relationship after relationship. One woman threatened to file attempted murder charges. That was enough to get Hegstrom's attention. He set out to find the root of his anger. He sought counseling. Most important, he met with God.

Little by little Hegstrom began rebuilding the relationships he'd destroyed. The process was long. Winning people's trust took time. Eventually his ex-wife fell in love with him again, and they were remarried.

Just as Jacob became Israel, the old Paul Hegstrom became a new man. His life took on a new direction. He began a ministry that helps men who are caught in the cycle of anger and abuse.[4]

In case I've been unclear, let me state the message of the Esau event: you can't move past your past without God's help. Apart from him, you will justify it, deny it, avoid it, or suppress it. But with God's help you can move forward.

It's time to do so. Let God speak over you the greatest of blessings: "Anyone who belongs to Christ has become a new person. The old life is gone; a new life has begun!" (2 Cor. 5:17 NLT).

You are no longer Jacob. You are Israel, and God fights for you.

You no longer swagger in false strength; you limp in God's power.

You need fear Esau no more. God has gone ahead of you. He has prepared the way and paved the path.

Your Esau, your past, is now your brother. Embrace him. And weep for joy.

# CHAPTER 10

# IN THE SHADOW OF SHECHEM

Genesis 34

**THERE'S NO WAY TO MAKE THIS CHAPTER A** pleasant one. No amount of makeup will cover the bruises. No amount of paint will conceal the rot. No amount of perfume will disguise the stink. A silk purse out of a sow's ear? Not doable.

So be advised. This event in the life of Jacob is raw. The Shechem incident involved a sexual predator, widespread deceit, sacrilege, bloodshed, and genocide. Hardly the stuff of a Sunday school lesson. But certainly the tragic stuff of life.

Scripture is straightforward about the ugly underbelly of human nature. Left to our own devices, the human heart is a wicked thing. And because it is, history bears witness to dreadful events like the slaughter at Shechem.

It's a jagged-edged story, this one. Crude as a stone knife.

Again, it's not easy to read, but the warning is hard to miss. *Don't settle for Shechem when the blessing is in Bethel.*

The command God gave Jacob in the homeland of Laban could hardly have been clearer. "I am the God who appeared to you at Bethel, where you poured olive oil on the stone you set up on end and where you made a promise to me. Now I want you to leave here and go back to the land where you were born" (Gen. 31:13 NCV).

The itinerary was singular: journey to Bethel. There was no need for a layover, no instruction to stop short of the destination. Jacob's daily to-do list contained one item: go to Bethel. Then how do we explain these two verses?

> Jacob left Northwest Mesopotamia and arrived safely at the city of Shechem in the land of Canaan. There he camped east of the city. He bought a part of the field where he had camped from the sons of Hamor father of Shechem for one hundred pieces of silver. (Gen. 33:18–19 NCV)

Shechem was only twenty miles from Bethel.[1] Jacob had covered five hundred miles since fleeing Laban. He was within eyeshot of his goal. But he stopped short.

Why did he pitch his tent in the shadow of Shechem? Archaeological digs indicate that Shechem at this point in history was "an imposing fortified city. [Its] walls enclosed a city of about six acres and therefore was probably occupied by between five hundred and a thousand people."[2] The city was an ancient commercial center at the crossroads of trade routes.

It's easy to imagine Jacob and his nomadic clan, weary from

travel, covered with road dust, thirsty for something other than water, and aching for conversation with someone other than family, deciding to pitch their tents. They stopped east of the Jordan in the highlands of Canaan. They met some Shechemites. They did some business. They made a few friends. They bought land.

He lived to regret each choice.

"At this time Dinah, the daughter of Leah and Jacob, went out to visit the women of the land" (Gen. 34:1 NCV). Dinah was around fifteen years of age.[3] She was Leah's seventh child, her youngest, and Jacob's only daughter.

The result was the worst possible outcome: "When Shechem son of Hamor the Hivite, the ruler of the land, saw her, he took her and forced her to have sexual relations with him" (Gen. 34:2 NCV).

Shechem was the son of the king. He bore the same name as the city. He was a scoundrel, a thug. His morals were lower than flounder droppings. Shechem kept Dinah in his house (v. 26). He became obsessed with her. He not only dishonored Jacob's daughter, he told his father, "Get me this young woman as a wife" (Gen. 34:4). Such words could only be spoken by a chauvinistic chump.

News of the rape reached Jacob. "But since his sons were out in the field with the cattle, Jacob said nothing until they came home" (Gen. 34:5 NCV). Jacob said nothing?! We expect a Mount Saint Helen's–level eruption. Not chilly apathy. Not cold callousness.

Dinah's brothers weren't so passive. When they heard what had happened, "they were very angry that Shechem had done such a wicked thing to Israel" (Gen. 34:7 NCV). This is the first use in Scripture of the name *Israel* to denote a community of people. The sons rightly saw the atrocity as an act against the people of God. Anger flashed in their eyes and pursed their lips.

Hamor, Shechem's father, made an offer to the brothers.

"My son Shechem is deeply in love with Dinah. Please let him marry her. Marry our people. Give your women to our men . . . take our women for your men . . . live in the same land with us . . . own land and . . . trade here."

"Shechem also talked to Jacob and to Dinah's brothers and said, 'Please accept my offer. I will give anything you ask.'" (8–11 NCV)

There was no apology. No expression of regret. No statement of remorse. Instead, Hamor appealed to the brothers' self-interest. You give Dinah to Shechem. We'll give women to you. Make marriages among all people. Lots of picnics and parties. One big happy family.

And Jacob? Silent as death. At no point did he defend Dinah's honor. We see no righteous anger. For goodness sake stand up for your daughter! Speak up for your family! Yet he did nothing. Was he actually considering intermarriage? Shechem was a Canaanite city! Jacob's train was off the track. Dare he dismiss this act of raw misogyny?

Jacob's sons didn't. Their sister had been sexually violated. They weren't going to sit by and do nothing. Simeon and Levi, blood brothers to Dinah, came forward with—what soon was apparent— one of the darkest and most nauseating plots in the Bible. They told Shechem and Hamor, "We cannot allow you to marry our sister, because you are not circumcised" (Gen. 34:14 NCV).

The act of circumcision was a holy deed, a designation of God's chosen people. It was a symbol of faith. Simeon and Levi did not have a ritual on their minds, however. They had revenge.

Hamor and Shechem approached the men "who went out of the gate of his city" (v. 24), meaning the men who went to war on behalf of Shechem.[4] They (astonishingly) convinced the soldiers to comply. They emphasized Jacob's lack of aggression and completely omitted Shechem's violation of Dinah. They promised financial windfall. "If we do this, their cattle and their animals will belong to us" (Gen. 34:23 NCV). Lust. Rape. Deceit. Greed. Is there any redeemable moment in this story?

Good luck in finding it.

"Every male in the city was circumcised" (Gen. 34:24 NIV).

Three days later, when the Shechemites were in the pain of healing, Simeon and Levi armed themselves with torches, knives, swords, and bludgeons. The boys of Jacob "took their swords and made a surprise attack on the city, killing all the men there" (Gen. 34:25 NCV).

No house was spared. The soldiers of Shechem were silenced. Wives and daughters wailed. Children wandered through the streets. The sons of Jacob were covered in blood. Simeon, Levi, and their gang plundered the city. They took women captive. They kidnapped children. They stole livestock. They ransacked the shops of the merchants and the homes of the innocents.

What a visceral, despicable act.

And Jacob? Did he interrupt the plot? Attempt to stop them? Did he upbraid his sons? Did he demand that they return the stolen goods? No. To the very end of this chapter Jacob was, well, so Jacob. The same cussedness that caused Jacob to take advantage of Esau, trick Isaac, neglect Leah—that same amnesia of God led him once again to think only of himself.

> Then Jacob said to Simeon and Levi, "You have caused me a lot of trouble. Now the Canaanites and the Perizzites who live in the land will hate me. Since there are only a few of us, if they join together to attack us, my people and I will be destroyed."
>
> But the brothers said, "We will not allow our sister to be treated like a prostitute." (Gen. 34:30–31 NCV)

Jacob placed his own safety higher than that of his daughter. In the end he was just as guilty as Shechem. As for Dinah, she never said a word. She was nothing more than a pawn in an alpha struggle.

And God? No one calls on him for wisdom. No one prays for strength. And, accordingly, Jacob is not called Israel. He has been given a new name, but he acts out of his old nature.

And so the story ends. What a distressing, depressing oil spill of a chapter. No heroes. No inspiration. It's not go-to material for feel-good sermons. Give us the Twenty-third Psalm. Give us the Sermon on the Mount. Give us Easter Sunday or Pentecost. We find inspiration in those events.

We find depravity in this one. Why is it included in Scripture?

Simple. We need the reminder. Apart from God's help, we are a disaster.

The human heart is a dark place. "Sin lurks deep in the hearts of the wicked, forever urging them on to evil deeds" (Ps. 36:1 TLB). "The heart is deceitful above all things and beyond cure. Who can understand it?" (Jer. 17:9 NIV).

The slain men of Shechem, the ruthlessness of the brothers, the blood of their butchery, the inertia of the father—they all combine to remind us of a fundamental message: When God is not sought, when the new nature is suppressed, when society submits to no one higher than self, the result is chaos. We become savages. We victimize the vulnerable. We break hearts, homes, covenants, and promises.

We create a poisoned system.

A poisoned system is one where people suppress their better selves and rise on the backs of others. It is one that awards power and force and downplays kindness and grace. Toxic cultures generate tribes and thrive on distrust. Societies like Shechem create underlings who appear less than human, undesirable, unworthy, and fearsome.

Shechem was a toxic culture.

Jacob and his sons inhaled the toxins.

Was it just a chapter ago that Jacob saw angels, wrestled with God, received a new name and a restored relationship with Esau? And now this. From the peak to the pit in the turn of a page.

How quickly the heart turns dark.

To be clear, in the Christian calculus, humanity is treasured, priceless, and destined for glory. We are created in God's image. We are endowed with fellowship and invited into eternal rest.

But we have squandered our inheritance by seeking to be God.

We have pitched our tent in the shadow of Shechem.

How else do we explain the corruption of the world? For all our medical and scientific advancements, for all our breakthroughs in technology and medicine, do we not battle the same inclinations as did our Bronze Age ancestors? Women are still objectified: almost one in three women worldwide, ages fifteen to forty-nine, is a victim of physical and/or sexual violence. One in three![5]

How is it that the twentieth century was the most murderous in history? Wars and genocides took more than 200 million victims in one hundred years! As we save more people than ever before, we find ways to slaughter more people than ever before. Consider the Sudanese massacre of the 1990s. The atrocities of Nanking, the Soviet Gulag, Auschwitz, and the Cambodian killing fields. The Rwandan bloodbath saw the deaths of more than 800,000 Tutsis in less than three months. "It was the equivalent of more than two World Trade Center slaughters every single day for one hundred days straight."[6]

According to Jesus this inclination to violence is not a problem of borders and broken treaties. It is a matter of the heart. "Out of the heart come evil thoughts—murder, adultery, sexual immorality, theft, false testimony, slander" (Matt. 15:19 NIV).

Heaven's assessment of the human condition is not a favorable one. In fact, it brings to mind a prognosis the doctor gave me five days ago.

Let me describe the setting in which I'm writing this chapter and see if you can guess the name of my affliction. I'm in a downstairs room of my house. I've ascended the stairs only for medicine and bedtime. I've had no face-to-face interaction with anyone but my wife, and she's wearing a hazmat suit.

Have you guessed it? Yep, COVID-19. At some point I inhaled a piece of a pandemic. My throat hurts. My body aches. My fever has spiked. My stomach churns. My name was added to the list I'd tried so hard to avoid.

We all struggle with an unseen, yet fatal, virus. Not of the body, but of the soul. Not COVID, but sin. We've all tested positive. We're all infected. Left untreated "the wages of sin is death" (Rom. 6:23 NIV).

It ruptures our relationship with God. Rather than seek him, we deny him. Rather than love his children, we hurt them.

But there is a treatment! These were the doctor's words to me five days ago. He'd scarcely told me that I was sick before he began telling me about something called immunotherapy. "We infuse you with antibodies. We regenerate your sick system with healthy cells."

If that's not an illustration of God's cure for sin, then I've misunderstood the meaning of the word *gospel.* Jesus took on our sin, our COVID-19 of the soul. He, the only virus-free being in human history, allowed himself to be infected with the human condition.

He took the punishment, and that made us whole.

Through his bruises we get healed. (Isa. 53:5 THE MESSAGE)

[Christ] never sinned, but he died for sinners to bring you safely home to God. (1 Peter 3:18 NLT)

In order to treat my infection, the physician attached me to an IV bag of healthy cells. In order to treat our sin, our Good Father infused and infuses us with the purest life: "It is no longer I who live," Paul proclaimed, "but Christ lives in me" (Gal. 2:20 NLT).

Coursing through the vein of the saint is the sinless, disease-blocking, life-giving transfusion of Christ. "The blood of Jesus . . . purifies us from all sin" (1 John 1:7 NIV).

God gives us what the doctor gave me: an honest assessment of my condition and a gracious provision to treat it.

But my doctor wasn't finished. "Lucado," he said, "if you want to get better, and if you don't want to spread this, you've got to get drastic. Quarantine for ten days."

So here I sit. Day five of utter boredom. Time passing slower than gums receding. But a serious condition calls for serious vigilance.

Doesn't sin require even more caution?

What is your Shechem? What temptation keeps you from Bethel? What voices seduce you? Distract you? Lure you away from your destiny?

To be clear, if you have the gift of Christ in your heart, you are set for life. Sin cannot destroy you. But it can trip you, ensnare you, entangle you. It cannot take your salvation, but it can take your joy, peace of mind, and rest.

Don't do what Jacob did. Don't engage in business where you have no business being. Get drastic. Walk a wide circle around the city. Shut off the internet. Give away your credit cards. Join AA. Cancel your trip to Vegas, New York City, or wherever it is you were planning to resort to your youth. Change your phone number. Break up with her. Stop seeing him. Don't pitch your tent in the shadow of Shechem.

> Above all else, guard your heart,
>     for everything you do flows from it.
> Keep your mouth free of perversity;
>     keep corrupt talk far from your lips.
> Let your eyes look straight ahead;
>     fix your gaze directly before you.

Give careful thought to the paths for your feet
    and be steadfast in all your ways.
Do not turn to the right or the left;
    keep your foot from evil. (Prov. 4:23–27 NIV)

Jacob got out. He realized that if they stayed, the Canaanites, who were much larger in number, would retaliate and kill his entire household. He pulled up stakes, loaded his camels, and turned toward Bethel. When he did, guess who was waiting for him? You've going to love the next chapter. To the degree that Shechem was sordid, Bethel was beautiful. But Jacob had to make a change.

Do likewise. Don't stop in Shechem when the blessing is in Bethel.

CHAPTER 11

# GRACE WILL BRING US HOME

Genesis 35

**SURELY GOD WAS DONE WITH JACOB.**

His season at Shechem was a toxic wasteland. Pitiless and inhuman. Jacob forgot who he was and what God had commanded. He was only twenty miles from Bethel, within a zip code of obedience. But he stopped short. His disobedience resulted in a devastated family. Rape. Carnage. Sacrilege.

Genesis 34 is the darkest chapter in the Jacob story. It's not that God was not present. It is that God was not sought. Jacob once again lived life by his own terms and paid a high price for doing so.

God has had his fill of the man, right? The flip-flopping fraud. What a sorry excuse for a patriarch. God will surely abandon him, turn away. And who could blame him? But that's not what happens.

Then God said to Jacob, "Go up to Bethel and settle there, and build an altar there to God, who appeared to you when you were fleeing from your brother Esau." (Gen. 35:1 NIV)

Instead of giving up on Jacob, God spoke to him! Directed him! God took the initiative. Whereas God is not mentioned in Genesis 34, his name appears, by my count, eleven times in the first fifteen verses of chapter 35. Jacob's tent was still pitched in the shadow of Shechem. Blood was under the fingernails of his sons. The stench of death was in the air. Jacob and his sons had behaved like the pagans who surrounded them.

Yet, God came to Jacob. And Jacob came to his senses.

So Jacob said to his household and to all who were with him, "Get rid of the foreign gods you have with you, and purify yourselves and change your clothes. Then come, let us go up to Bethel, where I will build an altar to God, who answered me in the day of my distress and who has been with me wherever I have gone." So they gave Jacob all the foreign gods they had and the rings in their ears, and Jacob buried them under the oak at Shechem. Then they set out, and the terror of God fell on the towns all around them so that no one pursued them. (Gen. 35:2–5 NIV)

Jacob had an Old Testament version of a come-to-Jesus moment. He reassumed the role of elder of the clan, leader of the family. No more false gods. No more flirting with Shechem. No more vacillating and waffling between convictions. Jacob resumed the journey home.

Yet, the hero of the hour was not Jacob. The hero was God. It was God who prompted Jacob, not Jacob who sought God. It was God who moved Jacob, not Jacob who moved God. It was God who stepped in, not Jacob who looked up. Jacob repented, yes. But only after God called out his name.

God not only stirred Jacob; he reminded him of his new name and of his promise to him.

> God said to him, "Your name is Jacob, but you will no longer be called Jacob; your name will be Israel." So he named him Israel.
>
> And God said to him, "I am God Almighty; be fruitful and increase in number. A nation and a community of nations will come from you, and kings will be among your descendants. The land I gave to Abraham and Isaac I also give to you, and I will give this land to your descendants after you." (Gen. 35:10–12 NIV)

Jacob forgot God over and over again, but God never once forgot Jacob. The One who promised to bless, blessed, and Jacob was confirmed, yet again, to be Israel.

Grace. All grace.

Could you use some?

Each day seems to bring a new way for us to wander off course. Anyone who tells you they haven't needs to read a book on honesty. The Christian life is not difficult; it is impossible. Need proof? Consider the Everest-level standard set in the Sermon on the Mount.

> "Whoever is angry with his brother without a cause shall be in danger of the judgment." (Matt. 5:22)

"Whoever looks at a woman to lust for her has already committed adultery with her in his heart." (v. 28)

"Whoever slaps you on your right cheek, turn the other to him also." (v. 39)

"Love your enemies, bless those who curse you." (v. 44)

I'm 0 for 4! Exactly how can we fulfill these commands?

Who has a chance? What hope do we have? The same hope that Jacob had. Grace. "Though sin is shown to be wide and deep, thank God his grace is wider and deeper still!" (Rom. 5:20 PHILLIPS).

Isn't that the great discovery? "He pre-destined us to be adopted by Himself as sons through Jesus Christ—such being His gracious will and pleasure" (Eph. 1:5 WNT). God moved you into his family. He changed your name, your address, and gave you a seat at the dinner table. You are "accepted in the Beloved" (Eph. 1:6).

A young woman once approached me after hearing a sermon on forgiveness. I was happy to see her and hear how she was doing. She had battled much rejection in her young life. But on this day she felt something different. "I've made a discovery."

"What?"

"I'm not an exception to acceptance."

Neither are you.

So for heaven's sake, accept your acceptance.

No more self-incrimination. No more self-accusation. No more self-condemnation. Make grace your permanent address. God has joined himself to you. You are "complete" (Col. 2:10).

You are "made right with God" (2 Cor. 5:21 NLT). You are "holy, and blameless, and above reproach" (Col. 1:22). "He has perfected for all time those who are being sanctified" (Heb. 10:14 ESV).

God has made a covenant to love you with an everlasting love, and he will keep it.

He did so with Jacob.

The old patriarch finally made it back to Bethel.

I wonder if he went on a search for the stone he'd used as a pillow. How long was he in Bethel before he told his wives that he'd need a backpack and a camel for the night? Did he meander around the desert in the fading light until he found the place where he saw the ladder? Did he rustle up a rock, lie on his back, and stare at the stars as the memory of the stairway came back to him? Did he reflect on the mess he'd made of his life? He'd cheated his brother. He'd swindled his nearly blind father. But in spite of it all, God had opened the heavens and lowered the celestial ladder so that Jacob would discover the greatest lesson of grace: God pursues us when we turn away from him.

In 1890 Francis Thompson, a Roman Catholic poet, described God as "The Hound of Heaven":

> I fled Him, down the nights and down the days;
> I fled Him, down the arches of the years;
> I fled Him, down the labyrinthine ways
>> Of my own mind; and in the mist of tears
> I hid from Him, and under running laughter.
>> Up vistaed hopes I sped;
>> And shot, precipitated,
> Adown Titanic glooms of chasmèd fears.[1]

Thompson speaks of Jesus as "this tremendous Lover" who pursues "with unhurrying chase, and unperturbed pace, deliberate speed, majestic instancy."

Would you open your heart to this possibility? God is wooing you, pursuing you, romancing you. Refuse him if you wish. Ignore him if you desire. Linger in the stench of Shechem for a time. But he will not give up. Did he not promise to lead you home? And has he ever broken a promise?

Not on your life.

This is the message of God, the aggressive promise of grace.

Trust it.

# CHAPTER 12

# DO YOU KNOW THIS GRACE?

**MY TO-DO LIST FOR MY FIRST DAY IN HEAVEN** reads as follows:

- Worship Jesus.
- Hug my dad, mom, brother, and sisters.
- Thank every person who prayed for me when I was a prodigal.
- Ask a few questions of the apostle Paul like, "What was that 'baptism for the dead' comment all about?"

And then I'd like to have a long conversation with Jacob. I'll make the quick walk to the Pearly Gate Sidewalk Café where he likes to spend his mornings. I'll introduce myself.

"Hello, Mr. Israel, I'm Max."

He'll look up from his latte and squint his eyes. He'll stroke his beard and tilt his head and—at least in my imagination—nod at the sound of my name.

"You're the guy who wrote the book about me, the grace book."

I'll blush, flattered that he would know about it.

"Yes."

"What was it? *God Never Gave Up on Jacob?*"

"*God Never Gives Up on You*," I'll say in perfect Hebrew.

"According to you, I was a train wreck of a patriarch."

"Well, you tricked your brother, lied to your father, tried to negotiate a deal with God, and that incident with Dinah at Shechem . . ."

"Okay, no need to rehash each event."

He will sigh and smile and ask me to sit with him. A crowd will gather at the sight of the woolly-haired man who still carries the staff that once served as a branch on a tree near the Jabbok River.

"What's on your mind, son?" he'll ask.

"Was I right to write what I wrote?"

"About me?"

"Yes."

"That God used me in spite of me and not because of me?"

"Yes."

"That I'm the poster child for the flawed and frauds?"

"How did you know the phrase 'poster child'?"

"Never mind that. You want to know if my story exists to billboard the grace of God?"

"I'd like to know your thoughts, yes."

"Well, here is my answer to your question . . ."

And then from a distance this husky voice, "Jacob! Jacob!"

He will look over my shoulder and say, "Esau! I forgot about our game. Excuse me, Max. But Esau and I have a tee time. We play Abraham and Isaac once a week. Let's finish this chat tomorrow."

And off he'll go. And I'll have to wait a day to hear his answer. And I'll have to wait to tell him what I'd like to say. Since I can't tell him, may I tell you?

"Jacob, your story is my story. Your life speaks to those of us who flounder and fail and flop. You invite us to believe in a grace that is so stunning, compelling, and convicting that we'd be fools to refuse it."

As I read and reread about Jacob, I continue to bump up against this certainty that God will bench him. Chalk it up to my Protestant, conservative upbringing. But each review of Jacob's story leaves me amazed at his seeming inability to shape up, clean up, and stand up for everything decent and moral.

He serpentined his way in and out of God's will. From Beersheba to Bethel. From heaven's ladder to Laban's clan. He tricked and was tricked. He twice saw angels and thrice heard the voice of God (Gen. 28:15; 32:28; 35:10). His name was changed, but his heart seemed less so. Why didn't God dismiss him? Replace him with someone more polished, more refined?

Yet, on the other hand I'm so grateful God didn't. I, too, game the system. I, too, am prone to pitch my tent in the shadow of Shechem. I've wrestled with God, daring to think my might and muscles would impress him. I can be smarmy, wormy, and less than straightforward.

I identify with Jacob. I limp.

I find great inspiration in the stories of other Bible heroes. Joseph and Daniel are wunderkinds and overachievers. The apostle John and Mary are the stuff of sages and mystics. The apostle Paul is the patron saint of the theologian and philosopher. But Jacob? He had a bit of Charlie Brown in him. Remember how Lucy assessed her friend?

"You, Charlie Brown, are a foul ball in the line drive of life! You're in the shadow of your own goal posts! You are a miscue! You are three putts on the eighteenth green! You are a seven-ten split in the tenth frame! You are a dropped rod and reel in the lake of life! You are a missed free throw, a shanked nine iron, and a called third strike!"[1]

We can only wonder how Lucy would have assessed Jacob.

His story exists for the times that the Jacob within us wonders, "Can God use a person like me?"

The answer, the reassuring and resounding answer, is "Yes."

Pure grace.

Grace is God's greatest idea. That he would treat us according to his heart and not ours. That he would see us and see his Son. That he would relentlessly attach himself to us in a love that no sin can sever. That he would swing the doors of heaven open to anyone who would trust, not impress, but trust him.

Amazing grace!

God does not stand on a ladder and tell us to climb it and find him. He lowers a ladder in the wilderness of our lives and finds us. He does not offer to use us if we behave. He pledges to use us, knowing all the while we will misbehave. Grace is not a gift for those who avoid the shadows of Shechem. Grace exists because none of us succeed in doing so.

God loving. God stooping. God offering. God caring and God carrying.

Do you know this grace?

Grace does for us what I did for my grandson. Denalyn and I were enjoying an afternoon chat when, from outside our back door, I heard these words: "Help! It's an emergency!"

I knew the voice because I know the girl. Rosie, our granddaughter. She was one month shy of six years, redheaded, blue-eyed, and in that moment sounded very urgent.

Rosie and her three-year-old brother, Max Wesley, were engaged in their favorite pastime, rock collecting. No need to spend money on toys for this duo. Just turn them loose in the open field behind our house so they can search for glittering, sparkly stones.

As we hurried out the back door, Jenna asked Rosie, "What happened?"

"Max can't stand up!"

I assumed the worst. Rattlesnake bite. A tumble into the ravine.

"Why can't he stand up?"

"He loaded rocks in his pockets. His pants fell down to his ankles. He's stuck and can't stand up."

We stopped, looked at each other, and smiled.

"Looks like a sermon illustration in the making," Denalyn told me.

She was right. It was an illustration deluxe. Little Max could not stand up. He was plopped on the path. His knees were drawn to his chest. His jeans were down to his ankles. The only thing separating his rear from the asphalt was Spiderman underwear.

"Can you get up?" I asked.

His voice was small and forlorn. "No."

"Can you try?"

When he did, the problem was all too clear. Each pocket was laden with rocks. Side pockets, rear pockets, all four pockets made heavy with stones.

"Do you need help?" I asked.

He said, "Yes." He let me help him remove the unnecessary loads one by one, rock by rock, weight by weight. Next thing you know he hitched up his jeans and began to play again.

(I told you it was a great illustration.)

What keeps you from rising up? What entangles your feet? What prevents you from moving forward? What load pilfers your peace?

Would you follow Max's example?

Max trusted us.

Won't you trust the grace of God?

Like Jacob, you struggle. Yet like Jacob, you are never disqualified by your struggles. "But we have this treasure in earthen vessels, that the excellence of the power may be of God and not of us" (2 Cor. 4:7).

Your treasure? A birthright. A spiritual heritage and destiny.

Yet these earthen vessels don't match our treasure. We have minds that wander. Bodies that age. Hearts that doubt. Eyes that lust. Convictions that crumble. We crack under pressure. Our porcelain has fissures. Who wants to use a broken vessel? God does. God does great things through brokenness. Broken soil gives crops. Broken eggs give life. Broken skies give rain. Broken crayons still color. Broken cocoons give flight. Broken alabaster jars give fragrance. The broken bread of the Eucharist gives hope. The broken body of Christ on the cross is the light of the world.

Which is precisely the point. God does great things through the greatly broken. It's not the strength of the vessel that matters; it's the strength of the One who can use it.

You are not the sum of your sins. You are the sum of Jesus' death, burial, and resurrection. You are as righteous as Jesus (2 Cor. 5:21). You "give off a sweet scent rising to God, which is recognized by those on the way of salvation—an aroma redolent with life" (2 Cor. 2:15 THE MESSAGE).

The ancient Japanese art of kintsugi is believed to have developed in the fifteenth century as a unique way to repair broken pottery. Sometimes translated as "golden journey," kintsugi repairs shattered pottery not by hiding the cracks but by highlighting them. The artist uses a lacquer of sorts to mend the fractures and then covers the adhesive with a fine gold or silver powder. The result? Something beautiful and unimagined with lines of gold and silver winding their way across the pottery. The piece then tells the story of its past with every crack and cranny, once hopelessly broken now gloriously redeemed by the artist.[2]

By the time we reach the end of Jacob's story, the old earthen vessel is held together by Elmer's glue and duct tape. Not much to look at, but he made it. "By faith Jacob, when he was dying, blessed each of the sons of Joseph, and worshiped, leaning on the top of his staff" (Heb. 11:21).

Jacob died worshipping. May the same be said about us.

We don't have to be strong to be saved. We don't have to be perfect to be redeemed. We don't have to score straight A's. We simply need to trust the God of Jacob, believe in a God who sticks with the unworthy and underachievers until we are safely home. He is the God of second chances and new beginnings. The God of grace.

And he never gives up on you.

# QUESTIONS
## FOR
## REFLECTION

---

PREPARED BY ANDREA LUCADO

# CHAPTER 1

# THE TILTED HALO SOCIETY

1. How would you describe the Tilted Halo Society?
    • Have you ever considered yourself a member of the Tilted Halo Society? Why or why not?
    • Do you tend to think of characters in the Bible as members of this society in the same way? Why or why not?

2. Fill in the blank: "Jacob, the _____ patriarch" (p. 4).
    • What did you know about Jacob before reading this book?
    • What surprised you about him after reading this chapter?

3. What was Jacob's nickname?
   - Do you know anyone like Jacob, someone who deserves a nickname like this?
   - How do you feel about this person?
   - Are you surprised that one of the patriarchs of the Jewish and Christian faiths was a person like this?

4. What was Jacob's family heritage? Who were his mother and father, grandmother and grandfather?
   - What do you know about Jacob's parents and grandparents?
   - How does our own heritage affect us, our actions, personalities, and faith?
   - Describe your heritage.
   - In what ways has your heritage affected your life, both positively and negatively?

5. Read Genesis 25:21–28.
   - How are we introduced to Jacob and Esau in Scripture? What was their relationship, even in the womb?
   - What was prophesied about Jacob and Esau? Why would this have been so surprising to Rebekah?
   - What was unusual about the birth of Jacob and Esau?
   - What symbolism is there in Jacob's holding on to his brother's heel?
   - How were Jacob and Esau different?
   - Which parent loved Jacob most? Which parent loved Esau most?
   - Why do you think this information is included in Scripture?

6. Max explains, "The firstborn of Isaac would be the next bearer of the covenant that God had made with Abraham." Read that covenant in Genesis 12:2–3.
    - How do we know God favored Abraham?
    - Why did he deserve to receive the covenant?
    - In what ways were Jacob and Abraham different?
    - Did Jacob deserve to carry on this covenant? Why or why not?

7. Jacob was not a prophet or a preacher. He fell short. He cheated. He lied.
    - If Jacob is the antihero of this story, who is the hero?
    - What theme is at the center of Jacob's story? (Hint: It's one word.)

8. How would you define *grace*?
    - How have you experienced grace in your life?
    - Where do you need to experience God's grace in your life now?

9. Even though you've just begun studying the life of Jacob, from what you know so far, in what way can you see yourself in his story?
    - Knowing how God felt about Jacob, how do you think he feels about you?
    - How can Jacob's story give you hope for your own story?

# CHAPTER 2

# FROM PRINCE TO PALOOKA

1. How do you handle times of waiting? Are you at peace or at odds? Perhaps it depends on the situation. Explain your response.
    • Max says, "Sin, at its root, is the unwillingness to wait" (p. 17). Do you agree with this statement? Why or why not?
    • Have you ever asked God to help you wait peacefully? Describe what happened and what you learned.

2. Read Genesis 25:29–34.
    • Why did Esau agree to sell his birthright to Jacob?
    • What did Esau's inability to wait in the moment cost him for a lifetime?

- Has your impatience ever cost you something important? What was the result?
- If you could relive that moment, what would you do?

3. Esau was not the only one in his family who had waiting issues. Read Genesis 27:1–29.
   - Rebekah knew God's prophecy about her sons. Still, she orchestrated this plan—a shortcut for Jacob to receive Isaac's blessing. Why do you think she insisted Jacob take this shortcut?
   - What was the result?

4. Read Genesis 27:41–45. What was the result of Jacob's and Rebekah's shortcut?
   - What did the shortcut achieve for Jacob?
   - What were the aftershocks of Jacob's action?
   - What do you think would have happened if Rebekah and Jacob had waited on the Lord?

5. Are you waiting on God for something right now?
   - How long have you been waiting?
   - Is there a difference between a shortcut and a helpful strategic move? How can you know the difference?

6. Whom do you identify with most in this chapter, and why?
   **Esau:** He was so desperate to fill his belly that he sold the most important thing in the world to him for a bowl of soup.

**Rebekah:** Even though she knew God's plan for her sons, she still took matters into her own hands and devised a plan that tore her family apart.

**Jacob:** He willingly participated in that plan to deceive his own father in order to gain status and prestige.

- How are Esau's, Rebekah's, and Jacob's stories cautionary tales for you as you're waiting on the Lord?
- How could their stories encourage you as you wait?

# CHAPTER 3

# LADDERS FROM HEAVEN

1. Describe a time when you were in deep despair.
   - What caused your despair?
   - Did you feel alone during this time? If so, why?
   - Did God feel near to you or far away? Why?
   - In this chapter you read about the long journey Jacob began alone. How could your experience with despair and loneliness help you empathize with Jacob? How do you think he was feeling when he left his home?

2. Read Genesis 28:10–19. What did Jacob see in his dream?
   - What do you believe about angels, and why?
   - According to Scripture, what role do angels play in our lives? (See Hebrews 1:14 and Psalm 91:11.)

- What role do angels play in our prayers? (Revelation 8:3–5)
- What do you think the angels represented in Jacob's dream?

3. What did Jacob hear in his dream?
   - What promises did God make to Jacob in his dream?
   - Max says, "There is . . . not one mention of Jacob in prayer, Jacob in faith, or Jacob in earnest pursuit of God" (p. 33). Considering this, what do these promises tell you about the character of God?

4. How have you heard the voice of God in your life? Was it a "Jacob's ladder" moment when you literally heard God's voice or a more indirect way of hearing God, maybe through a friend or through something you read or heard a person say?
   - What did God tell you?
   - Were you surprised to hear from God in that moment or in that way? Why or why not?
   - How have you seen God speak to others in your life?

5. Max says, "Grace does this. It pursues. Persists. Shows up and speaks up" (p. 34). Have you experienced grace in this way? If so, how?

6. How did Jacob respond to his dream?
   - What did he say, and what did he do?
   - When have you been surprised by God's presence during a dark or difficult time?

• How did God reveal himself to you?
• How did his presence affect you in that moment?

7. Fill in the blank: "Your ladder into heaven is not a vision. Yours is a person. _____ is our stairway" (p. 35).
   • How is Christ our "ladder"?
   • Do you tend to think of Jesus in this way—as your "go-between," as your "conduit through which blessings come and prayers ascend"? (p. 35). Why or why not?

8. Answer Max's question at the end of the chapter: "What is your version of a stone pillow?" (p. 36).
   • What is the promise of Jacob and Bethel? (p. 36).
   • How could this promise apply to your stone pillow?

9. Pillars are tangible reminders of faith. Jacob marked the place where he experienced God in his dream by building a small pillar and anointing it with oil. Why do you think he did this?
   • What physical markers or memorials are significant to you, and why?
   • What pillow-to-pillar moment in your life could you mark or memorialize?
   • Think about a way you could mark this moment or time in your life. What would your pillar look like? Where would you build it? How could you pray over it or anoint it?

CHAPTER 4

# NO QUID
# PRO QUO

1. Have you ever tried to bargain with God? If so, what was the nature of this bargain?
   - What gave you the courage to attempt a bargain with God?
   - What was the result?

2. Read Genesis 28:20–22.
   - Explain Jacob's attempt to bargain with God. What did Jacob ask God to do, and what would he exchange in the bargain?
   - How does Jacob's bargain with God differ from other biblical examples of bargaining with God? (Genesis 18:22–32 and 1 Samuel 1:11)

• How do you feel about Jacob's responding to his dream in this way?

3. Max quotes A. W. Tozer: "Left to ourselves we tend immediately to reduce God to manageable terms. We want to get Him where we can use Him or at least know where He is when we need Him. We want a God we can in some measure _____" (pp. 43–44). Fill in the blank.

    • How was Jacob's bargain an attempt to control God?

    • Do you see bargains you've made with God as attempts to control him? Why or why not?

    • Why do you think we try to control God? What do we hope the outcome will be?

4. Max talks about the couple he visited in the hospital after their daughter had been in an accident. Their faith was contingent upon their daughter getting well.

    • Have you ever felt this way?

    • Have you ever wanted or needed something so desperately that if God didn't give it to you, it would make you lose your faith?

    • Did God grant your request? If so, how did you respond? If not, how did you respond?

5. How are our bargains with God comparable to the ant farm Max describes in this chapter? (pp. 45–46)

    • How can this illustration give you perspective on how God feels about our offers?

6. What is the root of the word *hallowed,* used to describe God in Matthew 6:9?
   - What does this word mean?
   - What does this tell you about the nature of God?

7. Read the following verses:

"Let them know that you, whose name is the LORD—
> that you alone are the Most High over all the earth." (Psalm
> 83:18 NIV)

This is what the LORD says:

"Heaven is my throne,
> and the earth is my footstool.
Where is the house you will build for me?
> Where will my resting place be?
Has not my hand made all these things,
> and so they came into being?"
> declares the LORD. (Isaiah 66:1–2 NIV)

Then the LORD spoke to Job out of the storm. He said:

"Who is this that obscures my plans
> with words without knowledge?
Brace yourself like a man;
> I will question you,
> and you shall answer me.
"Where were you when I laid the earth's foundation?
> Tell me, if you understand.

Who marked off its dimensions? Surely you know!
    Who stretched a measuring line across it?
On what were its footings set,
    or who laid its cornerstone—
while the morning stars sang together
    and all the angels shouted for joy?
"Who shut up the sea behind doors
    when it burst forth from the womb,
when I made the clouds its garment
    and wrapped it in thick darkness,
when I fixed limits for it
    and set its doors and bars in place,
when I said, 'This far you may come and no farther . . .'" (Job
38:1–11 NIV)

- How do these verses describe God?
- How does this help you understand God's holiness, how
  he is set apart from us?

8. How do you reconcile this God with Jesus, one who was
   not apart from us but with us and near us?

9. Max says, "Prayer is not asking God to do what you want;
   it is trusting God to do what is best" (p. 48). What do you
   think of this statement?
   - What sorts of things do you request from God?
   - Do you think it's acceptable to pray for what you want?
     Why or why not?
   - Think of something you want right now, something

you've been asking God for. In light of this chapter, how could you bring this request to God?

10. Jacob's story is all about grace, despite his cheating, fumbling, selfish behavior. As Max says, "Jacob's story is a testimony to divine, unexpected, unrequested, undeserved kindness."
    - Do you believe Max's statement? Has it proven true in your own life?
    - Have you, like Jacob, tried to bargain with God? Have you witnessed that undeserved kindness from him? Explain.
    - How do you respond when bargaining with God doesn't bring the answer you wanted?

# CHAPTER 5

# THE TRICKSTER GETS TRICKED

1. Why did Rebekah send Jacob to the land of Haran? Why did
   *God* send Jacob to the land of Haran?

2. This chapter is about reaping what you sow. What has been
   your experience with reaping what you sow?
   • When have you sown something good? What was the
     result?
   • When have you sown something bad? What was the
     result?
   • What seeds had Jacob sown at this point in his story?

3. Read Genesis 29:1–13.
   • How was Jacob received by Laban and his family?
   • Why do you think Jacob wept when he met Rachel?

- What does this tell you about how Jacob was feeling after finally arriving in Haran?

4. Read Genesis 29:14–30.
   - How did Jacob feel about Rachel?
   - What was he willing to do for her?
   - What aspect of Jacob's character does this reveal?
   - What can we learn about Jacob's character, work ethic, or willpower from this story?

5. How did Laban's deception of Jacob mimic Jacob's deception of Isaac and Esau?
   - What lessons could Jacob have learned from this?
   - How do we know Jacob hadn't learned his lesson yet?
   - Why do you think this is?

6. What lessons have you learned from reaping what you sowed?
   - Like Jacob, do you find some lessons are tougher to learn than others? Do you keep sowing the same seed, expecting a different result? If so, how has this played out in your life?
   - What good seeds could you sow today to reap the benefits tomorrow?
   - Who else could benefit from these seeds?

7. Some say we get what we deserve. Oftentimes, as in the case of Jacob's story in this chapter, we do. But sometimes we don't. When have you *not* gotten what you "deserved"?

For example, you were a jerk to someone, but that person responded to you in a kind way. You turned the project in late, but your boss was gracious.

- How was grace at work in this scenario?
- Knowing we have God's unconditional love and unending grace through Christ, how do we balance this truth with the other truth Max presents: "You determine the quality of tomorrow by the seeds you sow today"? (p. 64)

8. How was grace present in Jacob's story with Rachel and Leah?

- Why do you think God didn't give up on Jacob as a part of his greater plan?
- Think of a moment when God extended grace to you. How did that experience impact your faith?
- Why do you think God hasn't given up on you?

# CHAPTER 6

# DOMESTIC TURF WARS

1. What do you know about your genealogy?
   - What is your family known for, good and bad?
   - Have you seen brokenness in your own family or witnessed it in a family you know?
   - How has this affected you?
   - How can brokenness affect a person's relationship with God?

2. Read Genesis 29:31–35.
   - Why did God enable Leah to conceive?
   - What was Leah's response to Reuben's birth?
   - What was her response to Simeon's birth?
   - What was her response to Levi's birth?
   - What was her response to Judah's birth?

- Use the chart below to fill in Leah's children—their names and the meaning of their names.
- Why do you think Leah praised God for the birth of Judah?
- How did Leah change from the time of Reuben's birth to Judah's?

3. Have you ever felt unseen or unloved as Leah did?
   - How did this lack of attention, affection, or love affect you?
   - Did God meet you in that place? If so, how?

4. Read Genesis 30:1–24.
   - Considering Rachel's plea to Jacob in verse 1, how do you think she felt about not being able to have children?
   - What was her solution?
   - Continue filling out the chart below with Zilpah's, Bilhah's, Leah's, and Rachel's children, their names, and the meaning of their names.

5. Max describes Rachel's and Leah's stories as "a case of two women, each longing for something they'd yet to find" (p. 74).
   - How did Rachel respond to her longing?
   - How did Rachel and Leah respond similarly and differently to their longings?
   - What have you longed for that you knew you couldn't have?
   - How did you react to this longing? What did you do to

get the thing you wanted, or what did you do while you waited for it?

- Why do these types of longings often bring out the worst in us?

6. What can you learn from Rachel and Leah about living with longing?

- What do their stories tell you about where God is in our longing and our waiting?
- How can this give you hope for what you long for?

7. What do you think Jacob, Rachel, and Leah's household was like?

- What tensions or rivalries did you experience in your family as you were growing up?
- What tensions or rivalries still exist today?
- How have these dynamics affected you and your family?

8. How did God use Jacob, Leah, and Rachel despite their dysfunction? What does this tell you about God and what he is capable of?

9. Max says, "Dysfunctional families can be used, even fixed" (p. 76). Do you believe this for your family? Why or why not?

- Max also says, "God delivers life through brokenness" (p. 75). When have you experienced this?
- If you have experienced brokenness in your own family or in a family you know, how could God deliver life

through that struggle? Spend time imagining what that healing could look like, how people could change, and how you could change. Even if it feels far-fetched, remember Jacob, Rachel, and Leah. How could their story give you hope for your story?

## JACOB'S CHILDREN

| Mother's Name | Child's Name | Meaning of Name |
|---|---|---|
| Leah | | |
| | | |
| | | |
| | | |
| | | |
| | | |
| Bilhah | | |
| | | |
| Zilpah | | |
| | | |
| Rachel | | |
| | | |

# CHAPTER 7

# LIFE WITH A LOUSE

1. Who is the Laban in your life? Your boss? A coworker? A family member or in-law? A Laban is someone you can't "escape." He or she is part of your life at least for the time being.
   - What Laban-like qualities does this person have?
   - How do you feel in this person's presence?
   - What kind of thoughts do you have about this person?

2. How did Laban treat Jacob? (Genesis 29:22–27; 30:31–36; 31:41–42)
   - How do you think Jacob felt about Laban?
   - Why do you think Laban treated Jacob this way?
   - Jacob worked for Laban for fourteen years. How long has your Laban been in your life?

- What do you think it was like for Jacob to have to live with and work for Laban for that many years?

3. Read Genesis 31:10–13.
   - What did God assure Jacob of in his dream?
   - Why do you think God waited until this moment to tell Jacob to leave?

4. In the dream God instructed Jacob to go back to his native land. In response Max says Jacob had two options: "trust God or grow anxious" (p. 81). What did Jacob decide to do? (See Genesis 31:3.)
   - How does this reflect a change in Jacob's heart and character?
   - Why do you think Jacob was willing to go back to his native land, the land he had fled in fear of his brother, Esau?

5. According to Genesis 30:27–28, why did Laban want Jacob to stay?
   - What impact did Jacob have on Laban?
   - What impact do you think you've had on your Laban? How has God blessed this person through you?
   - How does it feel to know that God blesses even the Labans of the world? Why do you feel this way?

6. Read Genesis 30:31–43.
   - How did Laban deceive Jacob once again?
   - How did Jacob respond?

- What was the result of Jacob's response?
- How did Jacob trust God even though he was deceived by Laban again?
- Have you ever been deceived or hurt by someone (maybe your Laban) and then given this person a second chance, only to be deceived or hurt again? Explain what happened.
- How did this affect your relationship with that person?

7. Read Hebrews 12:8–10:

This trouble you're in isn't punishment; it's *training*, the normal experience of children. Only irresponsible parents leave children to fend for themselves. Would you prefer an irresponsible God? We respect our own parents for training and not spoiling us, so why not embrace God's training so we can truly *live*? While we were children, our parents did what *seemed* best to them. But God is doing what *is* best for us, training us to live God's holy best. (THE MESSAGE)

- How is your Laban training you to do God's work and to better reflect his love?
- In chapter 5 we talked about how Laban's deception of Jacob mimicked Jacob's deception of Isaac and Esau. Sometimes our Labans are our Labans because we see a part of ourselves in them—something we don't like. Is this the case for your Laban? Does he or she have a characteristic you wish you didn't have? If so, what?

8. Read Genesis 31:38–42.
    - Whom does Jacob credit for his success while he worked for Laban?
    - How could this indicate another change in Jacob?

9. Max gives two pieces of advice for how to handle our Labans. Fill in the blanks: "___ to God about your Laban . . . ___ God for your Laban" (p. 88).
    - Have you ever talked to God about your Laban? Why or why not?
    - Have you ever thanked God for your Laban? Why or why not?
    - Spend some time talking to God about your Laban. Thank God for your Laban, even if it feels strange, even if you don't really mean it at first. Experiment with bringing gratitude into this relationship, and see how it changes not only the relationship, but you.

# CHAPTER 8

# FACE-TO-FACE WITH YOURSELF

1. How do you feel about Jacob at this point in the story? Do you like him or dislike him? Do you have hope for him or take pity on him? Why?

2. How do you think Jacob felt about returning to his native land and seeing Esau again?
    - What assurance did God give Jacob for this journey? (Genesis 31:3)
    - When have you known God's assurance in the face of a difficult conversation or confrontation?
    - Where did you go for this assurance? Prayer? Particular scriptures? Remembering God's faithfulness in other situations?

3. How did Jacob respond to God's assurance?
   - What does this tell you concerning how he felt about seeing Esau again?
   - Do you think Jacob felt genuine regret for what he had done to Esau, or do you think he was just afraid of Esau's anger? Explain your answer.

4. Read Jacob's prayer in Genesis 32:9–12.
   - How does Jacob praise God?
   - What does he ask for?
   - What does this tell you about how Jacob has changed?
   - What does this tell you about how Jacob was feeling about seeing Esau?

5. Read Genesis 32:22–30.
   - What thoughts or feelings arise when you read about Jacob's wrestling with the Stranger, or God, at Jabbok?
   - What point did God prove when he touched Jacob's hip?
   - Why do you think God waited until the end of the wrestling match to do this?

6. Think about a time you came face-to-face with yourself.
   - What events led to this moment?
   - How did you have to wrestle with God to get to this point?
   - Is there anything you need to face in yourself today that you've been avoiding? If so, what?
   - What do you need to believe about God to have this courage?

7. What did Jacob ask of God in verse 26?

   • What do you think of his request and of God's response?

   • Read John 14:13–14. Consider Jacob's request in light of these verses and their meaning for you.

8. What did God ask Jacob in verse 27?

   • If this Stranger was indeed God, he would have known Jacob's name. Why did he ask this anyway?

   • What does the name Israel mean?

   • How was the new Jacob (now named Israel) different from the old Jacob?

9. Once again our antihero experienced the grace of God in an unexpected way and in an unexpected place. What does this tell you about how God feels about your demons—the ones you've faced and the ones you have yet to face?

CHAPTER 9

# PAST TENSE

1. Fill in the blank: "To move forward into his future, Jacob had to come face-to-face with his ____" (p. 107).
   • What happened when Jacob faced his past?
   • Did this encounter change the future? How?

2. Read Genesis 33:1–3.
   • What does this tell you about how Jacob felt concerning his past with Esau?
   • What can you assume about the way Jacob presented his family and servants?

3. Read Genesis 33:4–11.
   • How did Esau respond to seeing Jacob?
   • How did he respond to Jacob's gifts?

- Why do you think Esau was able to embrace his brother?

4. Max lists several characters from the Bible who had stains on their pasts, including Moses, who murdered an Egyptian; Abraham, who lied about Sarah; Elijah, who was a coward; Esther, who didn't proclaim her faith; Peter, who was a betrayer; and Paul, who persecuted Christians. Of these, whose story resonates the most with you and why?
   - How did God use that person in the Bible?
   - If this person had allowed past mistakes to hold him or her back, what wouldn't have happened? Who wouldn't have been saved? What message would be missing from the Bible?

5. Is there something in your past you consider a "stain"?
   - Explain what past event or mistake feels like a stain to you.
   - How can you apply Jacob's story to erase what feels like a stain in your past?

6. How did God keep his promise to Jacob when he reunited with Esau? (See Genesis 28:15.)
   - What about this encounter surprises you?
   - What does God's promise-keeping say about grace?
   - If you believe God is with you in the same way he was with Jacob, what might change in the way you recall your past?

7. Romans 8:1–2 tells us: "Therefore, there is now no condemnation for those who are in Christ Jesus, because through Christ Jesus the law of the Spirit who gives life has set you free from the law of sin and death" (NIV).
   - Are you carrying a burden for something in your past?
   - Do you believe this scripture applies to you?

8. Read 1 John 1:9: "But if we confess our sins, he will forgive our sins, because we can trust God to do what is right. He will cleanse us from all the wrongs we have done" (NCV).
   - Why is confession entwined with God's grace?
   - What are the ways you can exercise confession?

9. Matthew 11:28–30 reminds us: "Come to Me, all who are weary and burdened, and I will give you rest. Take My yoke upon you and learn from Me, for I am gentle and humble in heart, and YOU WILL FIND REST FOR YOUR SOULS. For My yoke is comfortable and My burden is light" (NASB).
   - What comforting verses! Have you felt "burdened"?
   - What are some ways you've experienced the consolation offered in these verses?

# CHAPTER 10

# IN THE SHADOW OF SHECHEM

1. Max says, "Scripture is straightforward about the ugly underbelly of human nature" (p. 115).
   - Why do you think Scripture includes stories like the ones in this chapter?
   - What other Bible stories reveal truths about human nature?
   - How have you experienced the ugly underbelly of human nature in your life?

2. Read Genesis 31:13 and Genesis 33:12–20.
   - Where was Jacob instructed to go?
   - Where did he go instead?
   - What was the city of Shechem like? (p. 116)
   - Why did Jacob settle there rather than following Esau to their native land?

3. Read Genesis 34:1–12.
   • What did Jacob do when he found out Dinah had been raped by Shechem?
   • What did Dinah's brothers do?
   • What was Hamor's response?
   • What does each man's response tell you about how sexual assault and abuse were viewed during that time?

4. Read Genesis 34:18–23.
   • Why did Hamor, Shechem, and their men agree to be circumcised?
   • What does this tell you about the priorities of these men?

5. What is a "poisoned system"? (p. 121)
   • Have you ever found yourself in a poisoned system, such as a workplace, community, family, or church? How did being in this place affect you, your behavior, and your relationship with God?
   • How did staying in this place keep you from your Bethel—the place where you knew God wanted you to be?

6. Read Genesis 34:25–31.
   • How did Jacob's sons participate in the poisoned system of Shechem?
   • A terrible deed had been done to their sister. Do you think they were justified in their response? Why or why not?
   • What was Jacob's role in this part of the story?
   • Do you think this affected the brothers' actions?

7. Fill in the blanks: "To be clear, in the Christian calculus, humanity is _____, _____, and destined for _____. We are created in God's image. We are endowed with fellowship and invited into eternal rest. But we have squandered our inheritance by seeking to be _____" (pp. 121–122).
   • How can all of our sin be traced back to that one desire: to be God?
   • When have you sought to be God in your life?
   • What was the result?

8. Read the following verses:

   "Christ suffered for our sins once for all time. He never sinned, but he died for sinners to bring you safely home to God" (1 Peter 3:18 NLT).

   "But God demonstrates his own love for us in this: While we were still sinners, Christ died for us.

   "Since we have now been justified by his blood, how much more shall we be saved from God's wrath through him! For if, while we were God's enemies, we were reconciled to him through the death of his Son, how much more, having been reconciled, shall we be saved through his life!" (Romans 5:8–10 NIV)

   • What did Jesus do with the ugly underbelly of our human nature?
   • What does this mean for us today?

9. What Shechem do you need to get away from today? In other words, what or who tempts you, trips you up, or causes you to sin?

    • How could you take one step away from that place today?
    • How could you invite Christ into this process to give you courage and show you where you should go?

CHAPTER 11

# GRACE WILL BRING US HOME

1. When have you returned to your childhood home, or another home, after being away for a while?
   - How did you feel about the car, bus, or plane ride there?
   - Why is it sometimes difficult to return to places that were once home?

2. In Genesis 35:1, God instructed Jacob to return to Bethel. He was finally going home. On a separate piece of paper, list the major events in Jacob's life leading up to this return.
   - How did these events affect or change Jacob?
   - Who is he now compared to who he was when he fled from his home?
   - God had given this instruction to Jacob before, but he went to Shechem instead. Why do you think God gave Jacob a second chance?

3. Read Genesis 35:2–5.
   - What did Jacob instruct his household to do?
   - What did Jacob do with the foreign gods?
   - What could this symbolize for Jacob?

4. Burying the past is not always a negative thing. Sometimes we need to physically mark the fact that we are moving on and moving forward in life. Have you ever buried your past as Jacob did in Shechem?
   - How did you mark this event?
   - Or perhaps there's something from your past you need to bury. If so, what, and what could you do to physically mark the transition away from this memory, person, or place?

5. Read Genesis 35:9–13.
   - How did God bless Jacob?
   - Jacob was fickle. He vacillated between faithful and selfish. In the midst of Jacob's back-and-forth, how did God stay the same, and how is that proven by this passage?

6. When have you been fickle in your life, relationships, or faith?
   - Who in your life has remained constant, even as you've moved, aged, or changed?
   - What does this person mean to you?
   - Have you experienced this type of consistency from God? Why or why not?

- How does it feel to know that even when you've wavered in belief or have been caught up in sin, God was just as near to you as he was to Jacob, just as ready to offer you his grace and blessing?

7. It's one thing to understand the concept of God's grace. It's another to accept it for yourself. What holds you back from accepting God's grace for you, and why?
   - What would you need to believe about God to accept this grace once and for all?
   - What would you need to believe about yourself?

CHAPTER 12

# DO YOU KNOW THIS GRACE?

1. In one sentence how would you summarize Jacob's story?
   - What surprised you about Jacob in this book and in his story as it's recorded in Genesis?
   - What surprised you about God?

2. Max tells the story of his grandson, little Max, putting rocks in his pockets. He put in so many rocks he couldn't stand up. How can you relate to this story?
   - What rocks are weighing you down today? Past sin, regret, anxiety?
   - How long have these rocks been with you?

3. Read 2 Corinthians 4:7: "But we have this treasure in earthen vessels, that the excellence of the power may be of God and not of us" (NKJV).
   - What is our treasure?
   - What does your vessel look like? How has it been cracked and broken over the years?
   - What did Jacob's vessel look like? How was he broken?

4. Max describes an ancient Japanese art called kintsugi. What is it, and how is it an illustration of God's grace? (p. 143).
   - How did God repair Jacob's broken vessel?
   - Has God repaired some brokenness in your life, taking what was broken and turning it into something beautiful?
   - What brokenness in your life is still in need of repair?

5. Fill in the blanks: "You are not the sum of your _____. You are the sum of Jesus' _____, _____, and _____" (p. 143).

- How could you surrender to Christ the rocks you are carrying?
- How could the truth of Christ's death, burial, and resurrection repair the brokenness you feel today?

6. Read Genesis 35:27–29. What does this tell you about Jacob's relationship with Isaac and Esau?

7. Read Hebrews 11:21: "By faith Jacob, when he was dying, blessed each of the sons of Joseph, and worshiped."
   - Considering this along with Genesis 35:27–29, what kind of ending did Jacob's story have?
   - What kind of ending did Jacob *deserve*?
   - How do you feel about the ending he got?
   - How does this make you feel about your future and your own ending?

8. The title of this book is *God Never Gives Up on You*. After studying Jacob's life, how can you be confident that no matter what you've done or will do, God will never give up on you?

# NOTES

## Chapter 1: The Tilted Halo Society

1. Andrew E. Steinmann, *Genesis: An Introduction and Commentary*, Vol. 1, Tyndale Old Testament Commentaries (Downers Grove, IL: InterVarsity, 2019), 252; Gene A. Getz, *Jacob: Following God Without Looking Back* (Nashville, TN: Broadman & Holman, 1996), 8. "The term came to mean 'trip up, to engage in fraud.'"

2. See Isaiah 40:31.

3. See Genesis 47:28.

4. Craig Olson, "How Old Was Father Abraham? Reexamining the Patriarchal Lifespans in Light of Archaeology," https://www .academia.edu/33972456/How_Old_was_Father_Abraham_Re _examining_the_Patriarchal_Lifespans_in_Light_of_Archaeology, 13; Steinmann, *Genesis*, 252, 266.

5. See Genesis 12:1–5.

6. See Genesis 18:1–15.

7. Dennis Prager, *Genesis: God, Creation, and Destruction* (Washington D.C.: Regnery Faith, 2019), 241.

8. R. Kent Hughes, *Genesis: Beginning and Blessing* (Wheaton, IL: Crossway, 2004), 333; James Strong, *The New Strong's Expanded Exhaustive Concordance of the Bible* (Nashville, TN: Thomas Nelson, 2010), H7533—*râtsats*, which means to crush, smash, or crash together.

9. The beginnings of the Jewish people are recorded in Genesis 12:1–3. Abram (later Abraham) heard God call him to leave Mesopotamia for a land that would eventually be known as Israel. God promised to make a great people from Abram, to give him land, and to bless all the nations of the earth through him (see Gen. 18:17–18). This third blessing has been realized in part through the Jewish doctors, lawyers, diplomats, and scientists who have enhanced our lives. Yet in the New Testament the blessing of Abraham is given a name—Jesus Christ. In a sermon about Jesus, Peter declared: "These prophets, along with the covenant God made with your ancestors, are your family tree. God's covenant-word to Abraham provides the text: 'By your offspring all the families of the earth will be blessed.' But you are first in line: God, having raised up his Son, sent him to bless you as you turn, one by one, from your evil ways" (Acts 3:25–26 THE MESSAGE).

10. See Genesis 50:24; Exodus 3:15; Acts 7:32.

## Chapter 2: From Prince to Palooka

1. Eli Lizorkin-Eyzenberg, *The Hidden Story of Jacob: What We Can See in Hebrew That We Cannot See in English* (independently published, 2020), 11.

2. See Romans 9:12.

3. Isaac was about 135 years old when he blessed Jacob (Gen. 27). This can be determined by looking in the Scriptures. Jacob was 130 when he entered the land of Egypt (Gen. 47:9). The Scriptures say that Joseph, Jacob's son, was 39 at that time. Genesis 41:46 tells us Joseph was 30 when he entered Pharaoh's service in Egypt. Then there were 7 years of feast and 2 years of famine before Jacob came to Egypt (Gen. 45:4–11). We also know from the Scriptures that Jacob worked 14 years for two wives and then had Joseph (Gen. 29:20–28; 30:22–24). So 130 – 44 –14 = 72. Then allowing a couple of more years off for time for the pregnancy, Jacob was about 70 when he left home after the blessing. We also know that Isaac was 60 when Jacob was born (Gen. 25:26). This makes Isaac 135 (give or take) when he blessed Jacob. Adapted from https://homework.study.com/explanation/how-old-was-isaac -when-he-blessed-jacob-in-the-bible.html.

4. "Isaac had invoked Yahweh in pronouncing his blessing on Jacob

(see vv. 27–28), and one could not annul any words that called on God." Steinmann, *Genesis*, 270.

5. Steve Helling, "Lori Loughlin Speaks Out After Receiving 2-Month Prison Sentence: 'I Made an Awful Decision.'" *People*, August 21, 2020, people.com/crime/lori-loughlin-speaks-after -receiving-2-months-prison-sentence-i-made-an-awful-decision.

## Chapter 3: Ladders from Heaven

1. John H. Walton, *Genesis: The NIV Application Commentary* (Grand Rapids: Zondervan, 2001), 570.
2. Donald Grey Barnhouse, *Genesis: A Devotional Exposition* (Grand Rapids: Zondervan, 1971), 2:83.
3. R. Kent Hughes, *Genesis: Beginning and Blessing* (Wheaton, IL: Crossway, 2004), 359.
4. "Do you suppose that I cannot appeal to My Father, and He will immediately provide Me with more than twelve legions [more than 80,000] of angels?" (Matt. 26:53 AMPC).
5. Adapted from Jack Graham, *Angels: Who They Are, What They Do, and Why It Matters* (Minneapolis, MN: Bethany House, 2016), 111–12.
6. Hughes, *Genesis*, 361.

## Chapter 4: No Quid Pro Quo

1. A. W. Tozer, *The Knowledge of the Holy* (New York: HarperCollins, 1961), 8.
2. *Vine's Complete Expository Dictionary of Old and New Testament Words* (Nashville, TN: Thomas Nelson, 1985), 307.
3. Karl Barth, *Church Dogmatics*, vol. 2, part 2; 2 ed., trans. G. W. Bromiley, eds. G. W. Bromiley and T. F. Torrance (Edinburgh: T & T Clark, 1957), 685.
4. Paul David Tripp, *Awe: Why It Matters for Everything We Think, Say, and Do* (Wheaton, IL: Crossway, 2015), 73.

## Chapter 5: The Trickster Gets Tricked

1. See Ps. 37:15; Hab. 2:8; Ps. 7:15–16; Prov. 26:27; Eccles. 10:8; Ps. 9:15; Ps. 57:6; Prov. 28:10; 2 Peter 2:13; Ps. 35:8; Ps. 141:10; 1 Kings 8:32; 2 Chr. 6:23; Neh. 4:4; Jer. 50:15, 29; Ps. 140:9; Ps. 79:12; Ps. 137:8.

2. Lord Byron, "She Walks in Beauty," Poetry Foundation, https://www.poetryfoundation.org/poems/43844/she-walks-in-beauty.
3. "A kiss is a customary greeting among relatives." Bruce K. Waltke with Cathi J. Fredricks, *Genesis: A Commentary* (Grand Rapids: Zondervan, 2001), 401.
4. Nahum M. Sarna, *JPS Torah Commentary: Genesis* (Philadelphia: The Jewish Publication Society, 1989), 202, as quoted by R. Kent Hughes, *Genesis: Beginning and Blessing* (Wheaton, IL: Crossway, 2004), 367.
5. John H. Walton, *Genesis: The NIV Application Commentary* (Grand Rapids: Zondervan, 2001), 586.
6. Waltke, *Genesis*, 405.
7. Walton, *Genesis*, 586.
8. Waltke, *Genesis*, 405.
9. Waltke, Genesis, 406.
10. Natasha Geiling, "Step Inside the World's Most Dangerous Garden (If You Dare)," *Smithsonian Magazine*, September 22, 2014, https://www.smithsonianmag.com/travel/step-inside-worlds-most-dangerous-garden-if-you-dare-180952635/.

## Chapter 6: Domestic Turf Wars

1. Encyclopedia.com, s.v. "Mandrake," https://www.encyclopedia.com/plants-and-animals/plants/plants/mandrake.

## Chapter 7: Life with a Louse

1. This is a biblical principle. God prospered Pharaoh and blessed Egypt because of the presence of Joseph (Gen. 39–41). King Nebuchadnezzar became a believer because of the presence of Daniel (Dan. 4:34–37).
2. Andrew E. Steinmann, *Genesis: An Introduction and Commentary*, vol. 1, Tyndale Old Testament Commentaries (Downer's Grove, IL: IVP, 2019), 289.

## Chapter 8: Face-to-Face with Yourself

1. John R. Coats, *Original Sinners: A New Interpretation of Genesis* (New York: Free Press, 2009), 160.
2. Walter Brueggemann, *Genesis,* Interpretation, A Bible

Commentary for Teaching and Preaching (Louisville, KY: Westminster John Knox Press, 1982), 270.

3. *Israel* is a combination of two Hebrew words that mean "wrestle" (sarah) and "God" (el). It appears 2,431 times in the Bible, and there has been no shortage of discussion regarding its meaning. Some assume that Jacob received this name because he strove with God. Yet when "El" or "Jah," names of God, are used, God is always the doer. *Daniel* means "God judges." *Gabriel* means "God is my strength." The names of God describe the actions of God. See *Baker Theological Dictionary of the Bible,* Grand Rapids: Baker Books, 2000, p. 379 and Arthur W. Pink, *Gleanings in Genesis* (Chicago: Moody, 1950), 292. "There is some question about its meaning, though an educated guess about the original sense of the name would be: 'God will rule' or perhaps 'God will prevail.'" Robert Alter, *Genesis: Translation and Commentary* (New York: W. W. Norton, 1996), 182.

## Chapter 9: Past Tense

1. "Fred Snodgrass, 86, Dead Ball Player Muffed 1912 Fly," *New York Times*, April 6, 1974, https://www.nytimes.com/1974/04/06/archives/fred-snodgrass-86-dead-ball-player-muffed-1912-fly.html.

2. William Barclay, *The Acts of the Apostles*, rev. ed. (Philadelphia: Westminster, 1976), 64.

3. Steinmann, *Genesis*, 318.

4. Paul Hegstrom, *Angry Men and the Women Who Love Them: Breaking the Cycle of Physical and Emotional Abuse* (Kansas City: Beacon Hill, 1999) as quoted by John H. Walton, *Genesis: The NIV Application Commentary*, 566–67.

## Chapter 10: In the Shadow of Shechem

1. R. Kent Hughes, *Genesis: Beginning and Blessing* (Wheaton, IL: Crossway, 2004), 420.

2. John H. Walton, *Genesis: The NIV Application Commentary* (Grand Rapids, MI: Zondervan, 2001), 630.

3. Bruce K. Waltke with Cathi J. Fredricks, *Genesis: A Commentary* (Grand Rapids: Zondervan, 2001), 459.

4. Steinmann, *Genesis*, 325.

5. "Violence against Women," World Health Organization, March 9, 2021, https://www.who.int/news-room/fact-sheets/detail/violence-against-women.

6. Os Guinness, *Unspeakable: Facing Up to Evil in an Age of Genocide and Terror* (San Francisco: HarperCollins, 2005), 4–5.

## Chapter 11: Grace Will Bring Us Home

1. Francis Thompson, "The Hound of Heaven," *Complete Poetical Works of Francis Thompson* (New York: Oxford University Press, 1969), 89–94.

## Chapter 12: Do You Know This Grace?

1. PEANUTS©Peanuts Worldwide LLC. By ANDREWS MCMEEL SYNDICATION. Reprinted with permission. All rights reserved.

2. Kelly Richman-Abdou, "Kintsugi: The Centuries-Old Art of Repairing Broken Pottery with Gold," *My Modern Met*, March 5, 2022, mymodernmet.com/kintsugi-kintsukuroi.

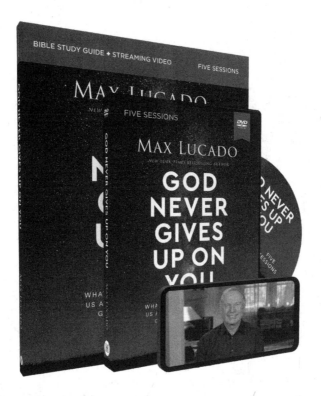

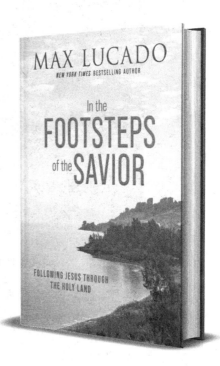

# MAX LUCADO
## BESTSELLERS

Anxious for Nothing

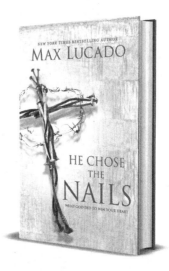

He Chose the Nails

Facing Your Giants

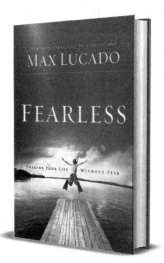

Fearless